DEC 13 '07

52.98
YBP

53023

D1256935

Student Companion to

William
FAULKNER

Recent Titles in
Student Companions to Classic Writers

Student Companion to

William
FAULKNER

John Dennis Anderson

Student Companions to Classic Writers

GREENWOOD PRESS
Westport, Connecticut • London

Library of Congress Cataloging-in-Publication Data

Anderson, John D. (John Dennis), 1954–
   Student companion to William Faulkner / John Dennis Anderson.
      p. cm.—(Student companions to classic writers, ISSN 1522–7979)
   Includes bibliographical references and index.
   ISBN 978–0–313–33439–9 (alk. paper)
   1. Faulkner, William, 1897–1962—Criticism and interpretation—Handbooks,
   manuals, etc. 2. Faulkner, William, 1897–1962—Examinations—Study guides.
   I. Title.
PS3511.A86Z577 2007
813'.52—dc22   2007025664

British Library Cataloguing in Publication Data is available.

Copyright © 2007 by John Dennis Anderson

All rights reserved. No portion of this book may be
reproduced, by any process or technique, without the
express written consent of the publisher.

Library of Congress Catalog Card Number: 2007025664
ISBN-13: 978–0–313–33439–9
ISSN: 1522–7979

First published in 2007

Greenwood Press, 88 Post Road West, Westport, CT 06881
An imprint of Greenwood Publishing Group, Inc.
www.greenwood.com

Printed in the United States of America

The paper used in this book complies with the
Permanent Paper Standard issued by the National
Information Standards Organization (Z39.48–1984).

10 9 8 7 6 5 4 3 2 1

For Peter and Lochinvar
"So faithful in love"

Contents

Series Foreword

This series has been designed to meet the needs of students and general readers for accessible literary criticism on the American and world writers most frequently studied and read in the secondary school, community college, and four-year college classrooms. Unlike other works of literary criticism that are written for the specialist and graduate student, or that feature a variety of reprinted scholarly essays on sometimes obscure aspects of the writer's work, the Student Companions to Classic Writers series is carefully crafted to examine each writer's major works fully and in a systematic way, at the level of the nonspecialist and general reader. The objective is to enable the reader to gain a deeper understanding of the work and to apply critical thinking skills to the act of reading. The proven format for the volumes in this series was developed by an advisory board of teachers and librarians for a successful series published by Greenwood Press, Critical Companions to Popular Contemporary Writers. Responding to their request for easy-to-use and yet challenging literary criticism for students and adult library patrons, Greenwood Press developed a systematic format that is not intimidating but helps the reader to develop the ability to analyze literature.

How does this work? Each volume in the Student Companions to Classic Writers series is written by a subject specialist, an academic who understands students' needs for basic and yet challenging examination of the writer's canon. Each volume begins with a biographical chapter, drawn from published sources, biographies, and autobiographies, that relates the writer's life to his or her work. The next chapter examines the writer's literary heritage, tracing the literary influences of other writers on that writer and explaining and discussing the literary genres into which the writer's work falls. Each of the following chapters examines a major work by the writer, those works most frequently read and studied by high school and college students. Depending on the writer's canon, generally between four and eight major works are examined, each in an individual chapter. The discussion of each work is organized into separate sections on plot development, character development, and major themes. Literary devices and style, narrative point of view, and historical setting are also discussed in turn if pertinent to the work. Each chapter concludes with an alternate critical perspective from which to read the work, such as a psychological or feminist criticism. The critical theory is defined briefly in easy, comprehensible language for the student. Looking at the literature from the point of view of a particular critical approach will help the reader to understand and apply critical theory to the act of reading and analyzing literature.

Of particular value in each volume is the bibliography, which includes a complete bibliography of the writer's works, a selected bibliography of biographical and critical works suitable for students, and lists of reviews of each work examined in the companion, both from the time the literature was originally published and from contemporary sources, all of which will be helpful to readers, teachers, and librarians who would like to consult additional sources.

As a source of literary criticism for the student or for the general reader, this series will help the reader to gain understanding of the writer's work and skill in critical reading.

Acknowledgments

This book was made possible by the support of the Arts and Humanities Council of Tulsa, Oklahoma, for a Chautauqua grant in 1995, and of Emerson College for a sabbatical leave in 2005–2006. Debra Adams of Greenwood Press provided patient and encouraging editorial guidance. My sister Cheryl Clark's resiliance has been an inspiration. I am grateful to Donnie Crenshaw for sharing with me his enthusiasm for William Faulkner's work, to Carolyn and Frank Kosewski for their loving support of their son-in-law, and, most of all, to Peter Kosewski for sharing the journey.

1

William Faulkner: A Southern Heart in Conflict with Itself

William Faulkner stated in his acceptance speech for the Nobel Prize for Literature that all that can make good writing is "the human heart in conflict with itself." Faulkner experienced major conflicts in his own life, including the competing demands of art and the marketplace and those of private and public life. He struggled much of his life for recognition as a writer, and he did eventually achieve fame as one of America's greatest authors when he won the 1949 Nobel Prize for Literature in 1950. Six years before, only one of his 17 books was still in print. Malcolm Cowley, a key figure in the revival of interest in Faulkner in the late 1940s, claimed that "Faulkner performed a labor of imagination that has not been equaled in our time," making "his story of Yoknapatawpha County stand as a parable or legend of all the Deep South" (Cowley, *Portable Faulkner* 2).

Faulkner lived his life deeply rooted in Lafayette County, Mississippi. In his body of work, he transformed his native land through masterful verbal art into the fictional Yoknapatawpha County. This "postage stamp" of land, of which he declared himself the "sole proprietor," is both a richly particularized emblem of the American South and a universal microcosm of humanity.

William Cuthbert Falkner (he added the *u* later) was born September 25, 1897, in New Albany, Mississippi, where his father Murry Falkner was a passenger agent for the family railroad. Faulkner shared his given name with his great-grandfather, William Clark Falkner (1825–1889), known as the Old Colonel, a colorful figure: soldier, author, banker, and railroad developer. In the Civil War, this illustrious forebear was elected Colonel of the 2nd Mississippi Infantry and fought conspicuously at the Battle of First Manassas. In 1889, he was killed in a duel immediately after being elected to the Mississippi legislature. The Old Colonel served as the prototype of Colonel John Sartoris in his great-grandson's Yoknapatawpha saga. An author as well, the Old Colonel also served as an inspiration for Faulkner's literary aspirations.

Faulkner was the oldest of four sons, and he remained close to his strong-willed and artistic mother, Maud Butler Falkner, throughout his life, only outliving her by two years. The family moved to Oxford, Mississippi, in Lafayette County in 1902 when Faulkner's grandfather (known as the Young Colonel) sold the family railroad. Thus losing a job he had loved, Faulkner's father turned to running a series of unsuccessful businesses (a livery stable, a coal-oil agency, and a hardware store) before finding employment in the business office of the University of Mississippi, his last job. Murry Falkner instilled in his son a love of horses and hunting, but his relationship with his oldest son was not as close as Maud's was with Billy (as Faulkner was called in his youth).

A second, important maternal influence on Faulkner was Caroline Barr, his black nanny whom the family called Mammy Callie. She came to work for the Falkners in 1902 and remained with William Faulkner until her death in 1940. Born a slave in the 1840s, Mammy Callie nurtured in him an understanding of the legacy of slavery and of the rich oral tradition that linked the past with the present. Faulkner would model his characters Dilsey Gibson in *The Sound and the Fury* and Molly Beauchamp in *Go Down, Moses* upon Mammy Callie; he delivered her eulogy in 1940.

Young Billy Faulkner dropped out of high school in Oxford (his lifelong home) in 1915, preferring to explore literature with his friend and mentor Phil Stone, who was four years older and a 1914 graduate of Yale. Stone introduced Faulkner to the Romantic poetry of Keats and Swinburne and the prose of such modernists as Conrad Aiken and Sherwood Anderson. When Stone returned to Yale to study law, Faulkner visited him there in 1918.

The trip north offered an escape for Faulkner from a disappointment in love. His childhood sweetheart, Estelle Oldham, had succumbed to family pressure and married Cornell Franklin in April of 1918. Distraught, Faulkner sought to enlist as a pilot in World War I. Rejected by the American military for being too short, he conspired with Phil Stone to pass himself off as English (with an assumed accent and the addition of *u* to his name) and to join the Royal Air Force in Canada. However, the war ended before he completed training. On his return to Oxford, he affected a limp that he claimed was the result of a plane crash (of which there is no evidence). As a special student, he took classes at the University of Mississippi, where his affectations of dress and manners earned him the nickname "Count No 'Count." He was acting out fictional personae, a talent he soon channeled into writing.

Faulkner's first publication was a poem in *The New Republic* in 1919. In this period he wrote poetry in the styles of T. S. Eliot and of the decadent French poets, as well as an experimental verse play, *The Marionettes*, that he also illustrated in imitation of Aubrey Beardsley. While writing this imitative apprentice work, he was content to support himself with odd jobs, such as selling books, painting houses, and working as a postmaster at the University of Mississippi who so neglected his job that he was asked to resign in 1924. He left for New Orleans and wrote sketches for the *Times-Picayune* and *The Double Dealer* to earn passage for a six-month trip to Europe in 1925, spent mostly in Paris, where modernist and cubist art fascinated him.

Faulkner's friends helped him get his early work published. With Phil Stone's help, Faulkner published a book of pastoral poems called *The Marble Faun* in 1924. Through Stone, Faulkner had met the writer Stark Young (also from Oxford), who had introduced him to Elizabeth Prall, the future wife of Sherwood Anderson, in New York in 1921. While visiting Prall in New Orleans in 1924, Faulkner became friends with Anderson, who encouraged the publishing house of Boni and Liveright to publish *Soldiers' Pay* (1926) and *Mosquitoes* (1927), satirical treatments of wounded veterans and bohemian artists, respectively. After the modest success of these books, Faulkner was dismayed when, in 1927, Horace Liveright flatly rejected his third novel, *Flags in the Dust*, about an aristocratic Southern family named Sartoris, saying it was too loosely plotted. Faulkner was so discouraged that he was close to abandoning his writing career: "I think now that I'll sell my typewriter and go to work—though God knows, it's sacrilege to waste that talent for idleness which I possess" (Blotner, *Selected Letters* 39).

Instead, he decided to write to suit only himself. "One day I seemed to shut a door," he later wrote, "between me and all publishers' addresses and book lists. I said to myself, Now I can write" ("Introduction for *The Sound and the Fury*" 227). The result was his favorite among his works, his "splendid failure," the novel that he wrote his "guts out" to produce, *The Sound and the Fury* (1929). Never again was the experience of writing to feel as ecstatic as it did to him with this tale of a beautiful doomed girl named Caddy, told from four points of view.

With his next novel, *As I Lay Dying* (1930), Faulkner was fully confident of his craft: "Sometimes technique charges in and takes command of the dream before the writer himself can get his hands on it. That is tour de force and the finished work is simply a matter of fitting bricks neatly together, since the writer knows probably every single word right to the end before he puts the first one down. This happened with *As I Lay Dying*" (Meriwether and Millgate 244). In his early thirties, Faulkner was a critical if not a commercial success as an exciting new voice in American literature.

Up to this point in Faulkner's life, his writing had been more of an avocation than a source of livelihood. However, he began to look to his writing as a source of income in 1929. The onset of the Great Depression that year also coincided with Faulkner's marriage to Estelle Oldham Franklin, now divorced and with two children. Faulkner's marriage to Estelle, which took place on June 20, 1929, was troubled from the beginning. Estelle, accustomed to a wealthy lifestyle and drinking heavily, made a half-hearted attempt at suicide during their bohemian honeymoon on the Gulf coast. Shouldering the responsibilities of a wife and two children, but encouraged by the lucrative sale of several stories to national magazines, Faulkner took a $6,000 mortgage on a faded antebellum mansion in April 1930. He chose the name Rowan Oak for the house, which he planned to restore with earnings from his pen.

Now the pressure was really on to write what would sell, while still retaining his artistic integrity. This tension was to strain his professional life for years to come, leading him to succumb to the lucrative temptations of Hollywood screenwriting and to risk his reputation on a lurid but literate gangster story of rape and degradation. *Sanctuary* (1930) created a sensation, selling more than all of Faulkner's previous books put together. In Oxford, it was so scandalous that Faulkner's father told an Ole Miss coed that it wasn't fit for a nice girl to read. His cousin Sallie Murry asked Faulkner, "Do you think up that material when you're drunk?" to which he replied, "Sallie Murry, I get a lot of it when I'm drunk." That fall in New York, Faulkner exercised his considerable capacity for alcohol as he was toasted by such literary lights as the wits of the Algonquin Round Table, a group of fashionably sophisticated writers that included Dorothy Parker and Robert Benchley. By this time, Faulkner had established a pattern of periodic binge drinking that posed a serious risk to his health.

Essentially a shy man, he drank in part to ease the pressures of social situations and of his difficult marriage to Estelle, also an alcoholic. The succès de scandale of *Sanctuary*, however, at least eased his financial pressures, although in an unexpected way. When silent pictures had given way to so-called talkies in the late 1920s, Hollywood studios began importing writers from the east to supply literate dialogue and stories.

Metro-Goldwyn-Mayer Studios offered Faulkner a contract for six weeks at $500 a week. He had just finished writing another major work, *Light in August,* and he was reluctant to go, but the publisher of *Sanctuary,* owing him $4,000 in royalties, was on the verge of bankruptcy. Behind in his mortgage payments, overdrawn at the bank, and unable to get credit, Faulkner headed for Hollywood.

Many of the stories about Faulkner in Hollywood have expanded in the telling until they have become as fictive as his novels. He enjoyed exaggerating his ignorance of movies and emphasizing the extravagance of the studio system. The truth is, though, that Faulkner worked hard as a screenwriter, writing thousands of pages of unproduced scripts as well as contributing to about fifty films (Kawin, *Faulkner and Film* 2–3). In the 1940s, Faulkner and the director Howard Hawks collaborated on *To Have and Have Not* (1944) and *The Big Sleep* (1946), both starring Humphrey Bogart and Lauren Bacall.

When Paramount bought the rights to *Sanctuary* in October of 1932, Faulkner cleared over $6,000 and headed back home to Oxford, where Hawks's influence allowed him to continue working on more screenplays from home, with occasional short stints in Hollywood. Faulkner also earned money by writing stories for high-paying glossy magazines such as *The Saturday Evening Post* (some later collected as *The Unvanquished* in 1938), but he felt ongoing pressure to provide financially for his extended family.

Enthusiastic about flying, Faulkner earned a pilot's license in 1933, bought a biplane, and encouraged his youngest brother Dean to become a pilot. In 1935, Faulkner published *Pylon,* a novel about barnstorming pilots. Then, on November 10, 1935, Dean was killed in a plane crash. Faulkner, devastated, blamed himself and sought solace first in whiskey and then by immersing himself in *Absalom, Absalom!,* his epic novel about the tragic Sutpen family in which Henry Sutpen kills his half-brother Charles Bon to prevent incest and miscegenation.

When money ran short again, Howard Hawks arranged for Faulkner to be put on a $1,000-a-week salary with Twentieth Century-Fox to work on a screenplay about World War I (which was to become the basis for *A Fable*). Back in California at the end of 1935, he met Meta Carpenter, Hawks's secretary and script girl, a lovely blonde from Mississippi. In a short time, they became lovers, a relationship that would continue intermittently for 15 years, to be followed in the 1950s by an affair between Faulkner and his young protégée Joan Williams. Faulkner's marriage to Estelle had improved briefly following the births of their two daughters. The first, Alabama, born in January 1931, had lived less than two weeks. The second,

Jill, born June 24, 1933, was Faulkner's "heart's darling (Blotner, *Faulkner* 318)." He could not risk losing her in a custody battle, and so he stayed with Estelle despite the bitterness of their differences.

Faulkner struggled to keep his fiction free of the taint of screenwriting. *Absalom, Absalom!* took Faulkner two years to finish. When it was finally done, early in January of 1936, Faulkner thought it was "the best novel yet written by an American" (Oates 138). Returning to Rowan Oak, he revised the manuscript and then binged on alcohol so badly that he had to dry out in a sanitarium in Byhalia, 50 miles north of Oxford, the first of many such detoxifications to come. His drinking was now beginning to endanger his ability to get work in Hollywood, but he took Estelle and three-year-old Jill there in July 1936. His love affair would suffer too. Meta realized that Faulkner would not divorce Estelle so she ended the affair and married Wolfgang Rebner. Meta's rejection fueled Faulkner's portrayal of a doomed love affair in the experimental work *The Wild Palms* (1939), which ironically juxtaposes the story of an intern whose lover dies as a result of a botched abortion at his hands with the tale of a convict rescuing a pregnant woman during a flood.

As the last year of the 1930s began, Faulkner's literary reputation seemed established. In January, along with John Steinbeck, he was elected to the National Institute of Arts and Letters, his picture was on the cover of *Time* magazine to mark the publication of *The Wild Palms*, and he was at work on *The Hamlet*—the first novel of a proposed trilogy about the Snopes family, a clan of greedy rednecks. However, these signs were misleading. In the 1940s, Faulkner's novels, except for *Sanctuary*, gradually went out of print, and he was increasingly unable to support himself and his extended family by writing fiction. The literary critical fashions of the 1930s had favored more socially-conscious, proletarian writers, such as John Steinbeck, Erskine Caldwell, and James T. Farrell. The Marxist-influenced critics of the 1930s, although admiring Faulkner's style, considered his work nihilistic and perverse. Desperate for money, but now notorious for his drinking, Faulkner reluctantly signed a seven-year contract with Warner Brothers at a third of his previous salary.

Between 1938 and 1942, Faulkner published three books that reworked previously published stories. *The Unvanquished* (1938) is a collection of linked stories of the Civil War that focused on the coming of age of young Bayard Sartoris and his black friend Ringo Strothers. *The Hamlet* (1940) is a comic novel of a rapacious clan of rednecks that became the first novel of the Snopes trilogy when followed much later by *The Town* (1957) and *The Mansion* (1959). *Go Down, Moses* (1942), Faulkner's most extensive treatment of race as a theme, was dedicated to Mammy Caroline Barr; it included "The Bear," a rite-of-passage story ranked with Faulkner's best work.

Released from Warner Brothers in 1946, Faulkner began in earnest to write A Fable, avowedly his "magnum o," an allegorical work about a Christ-like unknown soldier in World War I. This ultimately flawed book took him almost a decade to complete and marked a turn toward a more didactic, moralistic purpose to his fiction. In a break from toiling on A Fable, Faulkner dashed off Intruder in the Dust in 1948, a "mystery-murder" novel about race relations, "the premise being that the white people in the south, before the North or the govt. or anyone else, owe and must pay a responsibility to the Negro" (Blotner, Selected Letters 262). In a windfall for Faulkner, MGM bought the screen rights for $50,000 and shot the film on location in Oxford.

Intruder in the Dust presaged Faulkner's speaking out on integration. He argued in several public letters that southern blacks must receive equal rights, which led to Faulkner's being harassed and threatened by bigoted neighbors. However, his resistance to federal intervention to enforce those rights alienated staunch liberals. Faulkner's moderate liberalism angered everyone.

By 1950, though, Faulkner had become a Nobel Prize-winning writer for his body of work. He was recognized around the world as a chronicler of (as he stated in his Stockholm Address) "the old verities and truths of the heart, the old universal truths lacking which any story is ephemeral and doomed—love and honor and pity and pride and compassion and sacrifice" (Faulkner, Essays 120). The more conservative values of the post-war era contributed to a revival of interest in Faulkner's work, now perceived as mythic and universal rather than macabre and regional. The U.S. State Department sent him on a series of goodwill missions to South America, Europe, and Japan starting in 1954. To be near Jill and her family in Charlottesville, Faulkner accepted a position at the University of Virginia as writer-in-residence in 1957–58, an arrangement that continued in various forms for several years. Further honors Faulkner received included two National Book Awards (for his Collected Stories in 1951 and for A Fable in 1955) and the Legion of Honor of the Republic of France in 1951.

Another index of Faulkner's increasing fame was that his work was adapted for stage and screen. In 1951, Faulkner wrote an experimental novel partly in play form, Requiem for a Nun, a sequel to Sanctuary that extends the story of Temple Drake as a morality tale of suffering and redemption. A dramatic version adapted by Albert Camus was produced in Paris in 1956 and another version in New York in 1959. Hollywood film adaptations of his fiction made in the 1950s included The Sound and the

Fury, The Long Hot Summer (based on *The Hamlet*), and *The Tarnished Angels* (based on *Pylon*), although Faulkner declined to be involved in the productions. Also indicative of his popularity was that his final novel, *The Reivers*, a nostalgic look back at a turn-of-the-century Mississippi childhood, was chosen as a Book-of-the-Month Club selection.

The decade of the 1950s was a difficult one for Faulkner creatively and personally, in spite of his long-awaited fame and the money accompanying it. He feared aging and the loss of his potency as a man and a writer; his drinking binges periodically required treatment; he even apparently underwent electroshock therapy in 1952. In spite of these obstacles, he endured and prevailed, leaving a lasting legacy of stories of an enduring but changing South, struggling to come to terms with its mythic past. William Faulkner died of a heart attack July 6, 1962, at Wright's Sanitarium in Byhalia, Mississippi, where he had gone to recover from another alcoholic binge.

2

Faulkner's Literary Heritage

William Faulkner was heir to literary influences ranging from the regional to the international, and he wrote in a range of genres, most notably novels and short stories, but also including screenplays and apprentice work in poetry, which influenced his fiction in subtle but profound ways. He also negotiated in his work a complex tension between elite culture and popular culture, between highbrow and lowbrow appeals. His work has exerted immense influence on subsequent generations of writers.

William Faulkner inherited a dual and somewhat conflicted legacy from literary tradition—something old and something new—that he combined in making his distinctive contribution to literature. A descendant of the Southern oral tradition, he joined a long line of storytellers in recounting and passing on a rich legacy of myths and memories of the past. As a modernist, though, he experimented with form and technique to make a new literature consistent with the loss of certainty that is characteristic of modernism. Stephen M. Ross hears in Faulkner's style "a modernist angst garbed in Southern oratory's flowing rhetoric" (*Fiction's Inexhaustible Voice* x). According to David Minter, "Faulkner's imagination was in one of its aspects 'conservative' and . . . it was in another 'radical'" (*Faulkner's Questioning Narratives* 56). Minter sees these two aspects as twin commitments on the one hand to inherited stories and traditions and on the other to "a principle of playful experimentation in which repetition becomes a form of play and leads to and even merges with a commitment to revision, innovation, and re-creation" (58). The resulting body of work displays an ambivalent attitude toward tradition. Both reverential and revisionist in his fascination with the past, Faulkner combines a Romantic yearning for wholeness with a modernist embrace of fragmentation.

ORAL TRADITION

Faulkner grew up in a storytelling environment. "In his early years," as André Bleikasten explains, "Faulkner belonged to a community in which the telling and retelling of stories was still a major mode of social exchange and cultural transmission, the more cherished as after the Civil War recounting the Southern past had become the nostalgic memory-keeping and mythmaking of a defeated people" ("European Perspective" 89–90). His grandfather J.W.T. Falkner often told stories about his youth during the Civil War, stories about the Yankee patrols that would appear and take what they wanted and about the exploits of his father the Old Colonel. These tales steeped the young boy in the mystique of the Lost Cause of the Confederacy. J.W.T. Falkner (honorifically known as the Young Colonel even though he was never in the military) would occasionally host reunions of his father's partisan rangers and little Billy would hear their recountings of campaigns fought forty years before (Blotner, *Faulkner* 22). Billy and his brothers would enact the stories, just as he would eventually portray young Bayard Sartoris II (based somewhat on the Young Colonel) and Ringo at similar play in *The Unvanquished* (see chapter 3).

Other rich mines of stories included the men around the stove in Faulkner's father's livery stable, his great-aunt Alabama (the Young Colonel's sister), and the Negro blacksmith on his grandfather's farm. The greatest source of stories, though, was Mammy Callie, who told of her childhood as a slave (she was 16 when she was freed) and her memories of the dreaded Ku Klux Klan during Reconstruction, as well as ghost stories and animal tales. He noted how the same stories would be told in different versions, and he retained detailed memories of people, events, and even nuances of how the stories were told (Minter, *William Faulkner* 13). "Caroline Barr was not unique . . . as a source of stories and storytelling," notes Faulkner biographer Richard Gray. "She was, however, the most significant, intimate line of contact he had to the mixed history of his family and region, the tangled relations of black and white—and she offered the most immediate access possible to the oral tradition, the ingrained Southern preference for old tales and talking" (Gray 78). In his fiction, the intimacy of Faulkner's contact with storytellers appears in the way he often emphasizes telling and listening as themselves vividly lived experiences.

The oral tradition also shaped his use of language. He described his approach "studbook style" as "Southern Rhetoric out of Solitude" or "Oratory out of Solitude" (Cowley, *The Faulkner-Cowley File* 78). He wrote in the solitude of Oxford, away from the distractions of literary people, but he grew up and lived saturated in speech. He heard the sound of mesmerizing voices expansively talking, repeating and embellishing often-told stories. Accumulation of detail, repetition, and copiousness—these distinctive features of oral narrative—also characterize the "voiced" quality of Faulkner's prose, "its breathless, never-ending rush and rustle," as André Bleikasten describes it ("European Perspective" 88).

Another result of the influence of the oral tradition is evident in Faulkner's frequent use of oral storytelling frames in his fiction. "Much of the action of Faulkner's novels . . . consists of remembering and talking. In this way old tales and old tellings of them are evoked, preserved, and transmitted" (Minter, *Faulkner's Questioning Narratives* 57). Faulkner's work is full of references to voices, and some of his greatest novels (such as *The Sound and the Fury, As I Lay Dying,* and *Absalom, Absalom!*) are told by multiple narrators, placing the reader in the position of a listener who must reconcile the fragments and versions of the stories told.

Faulkner often revisited stories, telling them again in new contexts. In an interview, he stated "I'm a story-teller. I'm telling a story . . . to be repeated and retold" (Meriwether and Millgate 277). The differences between versions were sometimes contradictory, but Faulkner accepted these discrepancies as part of the uncertainty of the modern world. In his fiction, he shows how the understanding of reality is contingent upon multiple points of view. In this way, he reveals his modernist take on traditional storytelling.

Faulkner's friend Phil Stone introduced him to literary modernism around the time of World War I. Stone supplied "the future novelist with a necessary counterweight to the oral tradition inherited from Caroline Barr, great-aunt 'Bama and others. Faulkner's literary project grew out of the tension between the tradition of old tales and talking he took from his region and the disruptive techniques of modernism" (Gray 78). Faulkner is thus both firmly rooted in his region and a part of the international modernist movement.

FAULKNER AS MODERNIST

Although Faulkner is often labeled a modernist, there is much critical debate about definitions of modernism and, thus, about how Faulkner's work manifests it. Debrah Raschke emphasizes the experience of loss as the essence of modernism. She argues that the accelerated pace of change resulting from the Industrial Revolution created a breeding ground for a modernist sensibility that took shape in the early twentieth century. Rapid social change was reflected in the radically new scientific and psychological theories of Darwin and Freud. Their theories of evolution and psychoanalysis challenged long-established beliefs about the self and individual autonomy, creating a crisis of knowledge and a loss of certainty in the realms of metaphysics, theology, and aesthetics. With this loss of certainty came the death of God and the disappearance of the omniscient author, according to Ian Watt. The impact on literature of these losses was expressed in the work of writers such as James Joyce, Virginia Woolf, and T. S. Eliot, who are labeled with Faulkner as high modernists.

Faulkner expresses the loss of certainty, Raschke says, in terms of breakdowns of meaning, structure, and origin, putting the reader in the position of seeking to integrate what is broken. On the level of the self, such characters as Quentin Compson in *The Sound and the Fury*, Darl Bundren in *As I Lay Dying*, and Joe Christmas in *Light in August* lack coherent identities and feel isolated and fragmented. Through such modernist techniques as stream of consciousness, interior monologues, and multiple narrative points of view, Faulkner denies these characters a firm ground of narrative authority, and the reader shares their disrupted subjectivities. These techniques thus convey a loss of coherence in terms of both content and form.

Stream of consciousness (a term coined by the philosopher William James) refers to the recording of the flow of a character's thoughts in a fragmentary, nonlinear manner. Images and impressions suggest others through an associative process that ignores distinctions between past, present, and future. Robert Humphrey points out that stream-of-consciousness techniques encompass various levels or degrees of consciousness, ranging from unconscious, preverbal depths to levels of conscious verbalization, whether written or spoken. Presentation of character via images that stream through consciousness matched the modernist concept of incoherent and fragmented selfhood.

Interior monologues and multiple points of view further isolate and fragment how readers experience and perceive characters in modernist literature. The Compson brothers in *The Sound and the Fury* and the Bundren family in *As I Lay Dying* are presented as locked in their interior monologues as if imprisoned in cells of the self. In *Absalom, Absalom!* Faulkner creates an echo chamber of versions of the Sutpen family narrated by a series of speakers with variously biased points of view. In *Light in August*, as well (even though Faulkner employs a third-person narrator), he compartmentalizes the characters around Joe Christmas (Kartiganer qtd. in

Raschke 112). The techniques of interior monologues and multiple points of view reinforce the modernist loss of certainty.

Faulkner's literary roots also sink deeper than modernism's attempt to "make it new." Though he often claimed to be just a farmer who liked to write and not a literary man, he read widely and deeply in the classics of European literature. Faulkner often acknowledged his admiration for the Old Testament, Shakespeare, Dickens, and Conrad. Speaking of Balzac, another writer he respected, Faulkner credited him with creating "an intact world of his own, a bloodstream running through twenty books" (Meriwether and Millgate 251), a statement that applies as well to Faulkner's Yoknapatawpha cycle. On several occasions, Faulkner mentioned that he frequently re-read Cervantes's *Don Quixote*, Melville's *Moby-Dick*, Twain's *Huckleberry Finn*, Dostoevsky's *The Brothers Karamazov*, and Flaubert's *Madame Bovary*. In spite of his denial of being literary, his work reveals the influences of these novels, which he thought of as old friends.

GENRE: ELITE VS. POPULAR

Although he is best known as a novelist, Faulkner first aspired to write poetry, and he honed his craft by imitating Romantic poets such as John Keats and Percy Shelley, the French decadents Jules Laforgue, Paul Verlaine, and Stephane Mallarmé, and the modernists T. S. Eliot and Conrad Aiken (Sensibar). "I think that every novelist is a failed poet," he told an interviewer. "I think he tries to write poetry first, then finds he can't. Then he tries the short story, which is the most demanding form after poetry. And failing at that, only then does he take up novel-writing" (Meriwether and Millgate 217). In the early 1920s, while staying in New Orleans, Faulkner began to write experimental, impressionistic prose sketches that he published in the magazine *The Double Dealer* and the newspaper *The Times-Picayune*. In this way, Faulkner made the transition from poetry to prose and began his struggle with the conflict between writing literature that would appeal to a discerning few versus producing commercial fiction and screenplays for a wide popular market.

Faulkner's best and most significant works are the novels discussed in chapters 4 through 7—novels that were not bestsellers, but enjoyed critical respect when first published and are now considered canonical masterpieces of world literature. In writing them, Faulkner aimed for artistic standards beyond what merely would sell to something worthy of standing beside Shakespeare and Dickens and Dostoevsky. Clearly, though, Faulkner wanted his writing to reach a wide audience, and he was aware of pressures to write formulaic work that he called trash, such as stories for glossy magazines, movie scripts, and bestselling novels. However, when he did write what he thought would sell, his work often pushed the envelope of these conventional genres, subverting expectations and blurring the supposedly rigid boundary between literary and commercial forms.

In between and even while writing his greatest novels, Faulkner often paused to "stir the pot," as he called writing fiction that would produce income. He claimed to have written his novel *Sanctuary* to appeal to readers interested in sensational fiction about sex and crime. However, he also admitted that he paid his publisher for the costs of extensively revising it after it had been typeset in order to make of it a work that would not embarrass *The Sound and the Fury*. Even when stooping to write something sensational, he wrote a remarkable, complex book that explored the nature of evil.

Similarly, Faulkner wrote the stories that became the novel *The Unvanquished* to appeal to the middlebrow readers of the well-paying magazine the *Saturday Evening Post*. who expected stories about the Civil War to adhere to conventional formulas of heroism. Then, when he revised them for publication as a book and added the concluding story, he subtly subverted those expectations. In her article "Dismantling the *Saturday Evening Post* Reader," Susan Donaldson observes that

> Indeed, the last story, "An Odor of Verbena," and the passages added to the preceding stories in *The Unvanquished* imply that reader expectations attuned to tales of adventure and glory can be misleading and even dangerously blind to the rigid codification of storybook legends. . . . In [these] tales about revenge during the Civil War and Reconstruction, Faulkner managed to wreak his own special brand of vengeance on the *Saturday Evening Post,* a magazine that rejected far more of his stories than it ever published. (180)

An additional benefit for Faulkner in the case of *The Unvanquished* was the sale of the screen rights for $25,000 in 1938.

Also reflecting the influence of popular culture is Faulkner's novel *If I Forget Thee, Jerusalem,* which was published in 1939 as *The Wild Palms.* The novel alternates between two unrelated stories, "The Wild Palms" and "Old Man"; the former involves a tragic love affair between a couple as they wander from New Orleans to Chicago, Utah, and the Gulf Coast in 1937 until the woman, Charlotte Rittenmeyer, dies from a botched abortion performed by her lover Harry Wilbourne. "Old Man" tells of a prisoner known only as the Tall Convict rescuing a pregnant woman during the great Mississippi River flood of 1927 (see chapter 8). According to Anne Goodwyn Jones, the half of the novel entitled "The Wild

Palms" uses a plot structure from popular romance fiction, told from a masculine point of view with a weak hero and a sad ending that makes it a "bad romance" in Janice Radway's terms. "[T]his is a masculine popular romance plot, a plot written by men for men, a plot that derives specifically from male fears [of women] and that attempts to warn men away from the dangers it articulates" (Jones, "The Kotex Age" 156). Jones makes the point that Faulkner's modernist tendencies influenced him to think of "art, which was original, individual, and good" as separate from "popular culture, which was slavishly imitative, mass-produced, and bad" (144). Yet, *If I Forget Thee, Jerusalem* "shows signs at least of stepping aside from this conventional dichotomy. The novel is thick with allusions to both high and popular culture. . . . [The] effect is to raise questions about the *reasons* for the difference between pop and high culture, and still more to comment on the motivation and effects of stories of any kind" (145).

Faulkner spurned mass culture, but he was dependent upon it financially, and his work addressed and responded to it. In various ways, Faulkner negotiated the complex tension between the demands of art and commerce in the market for fiction.

SCREENWRITING

Faulkner felt this conflict most intensely when he was offered work in Hollywood. Starting in May 1932, Faulkner worked off and on for 22 years for such major studios as Metro-Goldwyn-Mayer, Twentieth Century-Fox, and Warner Brothers. He called these stints sojourns "downriver," likening working under contract in Hollywood to being sold as a slave into the deepest South, where the conditions of slavery were harshest (Blotner, *Selected Letters* 72). Faulkner worked conscientiously on many film scripts, although he only received screen credit on six films, including the two films starring Humphrey Bogart and Lauren Bacall mentioned in chapter 1.

His success in Hollywood, modest enough, was largely due to the director Howard Hawks, who shared Faulkner's interests in hunting and aviation and who encouraged the studios to buy the screen rights to his fiction and to hire him as a screenwriter (Dardis 94). Starting at $500 a week and working up to as much as $1,000 a week in 1934 and 1935—the height of the Great Depression—Faulkner was extremely well paid at that time. Also, in 1932, he received $2,250 for the rights to his story "Turnabout" (which he co-adapted for the screen and Howard Hawks directed as the film *Today We Live*) and $6,000 for the rights to *Sanctuary* (filmed as *The*

Story of Temple Drake). The two films were released within a month of each other in 1933. In the 1940s, though, financial need forced Faulkner to accept an unappealing seven-year contract for $300 a week, a junior writer's salary (Dardis 118).

Bruce Kawin, who has made a close study of Faulkner's contributions to film, notes the paradox that "Faulkner's novels are cinematic, and his screenplays are novelistic" (Kawin, *Faulkner and Film* 13). His screenwriting, influenced by Hawks, was straightforward, telling single stories using few flashbacks or montage effects (dynamically juxtaposed images). In his fiction, however, he interweaves multiple stories, mixes up chronology, and uses stream-of-consciousness techniques. Yet Kawin argues that Faulkner's screenwriting remains a significant part of his body of work. "Some of his scripts have the virtues of his better short stories; most are interesting for the skeletal way they reveal Faulkner's sense of tragic form or for their abbreviated indications of some of the ways he saw love, honor, sacrifice, and sublimated incest" (Kawin, *Faulkner's MGM Screenplays* xiv).

Conversely, some of Faulkner's less highly regarded fiction reveals the influence of Hollywood. *Pylon* (1935), for example, contains elements of characterization and style reminiscent of Hawks's films. One of Faulkner's few novels not set in Yoknapatawpha County, *Pylon* takes place in a thinly disguised version of New Orleans called New Valois during Mardi Gras. "Only [Faulkner's] recent involvement with Hawks and Hollywood can explain his ever having written such a book" about high-speed racing pilots, according to Tom Dardis (99). He notes the similarity of the emphasis in *Pylon* on the dangers of flying and speed with that in Hawks's films and the likeness of Faulkner's central female character Laverne Shumann to tough women in such Hawks films as *To Have and Have Not* and *His Girl Friday*. The way in which Faulkner juxtaposes two unrelated stories in *The Wild Palms* (1938) reminds Bruce Kawin of the cinematic concept of montage (Kawin, *Faulkner and Film*).

FAULKNER'S LEGACY

Faulkner's fellow Mississippi writer Eudora Welty likened his presence in the state to living near a big mountain (Welty 9). Faulkner's work has exercised such a pervasive and continuing influence on subsequent writers that the adjective *Faulknerian* is a common term for a recognizable style, structure, or subject in fiction. Cormac McCarthy's early work, such as *All The Pretty Horses*, has often been described as Faulknerian in style; playwright Horton Foote's nine-play *Orphans' Home Cycle*, along with other plays set in his fictional Harrison, Texas, are often labeled Faulknerian in their scope and sense of place. Faulkner's work is so overpowering a part of the literary landscape that writers sometimes respond to the anxiety of his influence by resisting it. Among the most prominent and representative (and resisting) of his literary heirs are two fellow Nobel Prize winners: the African American writer Toni Morrison (author of *The Bluest Eye, Song of Solomon*, and *Beloved*) and the Latin American writer Gabriel García Márquez (author of *One Hundred Years of Solitude* and *Leaf Storm*).

Toni Morrison has acknowledged spending a great deal of time thinking about Faulkner and his enormous effect on her, notably in his focus on a particular, localized world. Yet she also, as a black woman writer from Ohio, emphasizes her differences from him. Comparisons of the two writers have resulted in insightful analyses in Philip Weinstein's book *What Else But Love? The Ordeal of Race in Faulkner and Morrison* and in the collection of essays *Unflinching Gaze: Morrison and Faulkner Re-Envisioned* (Kolmerten et al.). John N. Duvall's essay in the collection, for example, argues that Faulkner and Morrison both create characters that are outcasts or pariahs who form alternative social groupings. In Faulkner's work, these so-called marginal couples (such as Joe Christmas and Joanna Burden in *Light in August*) disrupt traditional gender roles; in Morrison's novels such as *Sula* and *Beloved*, trios of women form alternative nuclear families. Despite Morrison's ambivalence about being compared to Faulkner, she acknowledges his effect on her.

Similarly, Gabriel García Márquez grants that Faulkner "is present in all the novels of Latin America. . . . The Faulknerian method is very effective for relating Latin American reality" (qtd. in Frisch 222). Yet he also says "His influence has screwed me up" (qtd. in Oakley 408). Helen Oakley argues that the U.S. government's promotion in Latin America in the 1950s of Faulkner's work as part of Cold War propaganda efforts complicated the efforts of Latin American writers to establish their own individual identities (408). Regardless of the ambivalence of García Márquez, Faulkner's impact on Latin American literature has been profound. Sparked in part, according to Ilan Stavans, by a superb translation of *The Wild Palms* by Jorge Luis Borges, who "mimicked the American's style elegantly, making it fluid, electrifying, breathtaking in Spanish," Faulkner's work strongly influenced Juan Carlos Onetti in Uruguay, Juan Rulfo in Mexico, and Gabriel García Márquez in Colombia (500). Writers such as the Mexican Carlos Fuentes and the Peruvian Mario Vargas Llosa were struck by Faulkner's depiction of the processes of social change that the American South shared with the Latin America.

A major figure in American and world literature, William Faulkner combined traditional Southern orality with dazzling modernist technique and sense of loss in his fabled Yoknapatawpha County. He juggled modernist notions of high art with the lure of popular culture in ways that complicated the simplistic dichotomy of the two spheres. As a transition into the stratosphere of his four towering masterpieces, *The Sound and the Fury, As I Lay Dying, Light in August*, and *Absalom, Absalom!* I turn first to the more modest but accessible achievement of *The Unvanquished*.

3

The Unvanquished (1938) and *Sartoris* (1929)

William Faulkner's third and ninth novels together provide a good introduction to his body of work. *Sartoris* (1929) and *The Unvanquished* (1938) are related novels that share the Yoknapatawpha setting for which he is best known and cover different stages of the life of the same character, Bayard Sartoris II.

Faulkner sometimes encouraged readers unfamiliar with his work to start with *The Unvanquished* (Gwynn and Blotner 2). Most critics have considered it conventional and hence inferior to Faulkner's major work; he wrote most of it as a series of stories for the slick, popular magazine *The Saturday Evening Post*. Faulkner himself referred to the stories, in a letter to his agent, as trash. He didn't care who bought it "as long as they pay the best price I can get" (Blotner, *Selected Letters* 84). However, the novel serves as an excellent place to begin to read Faulkner because it is told more straightforwardly than his more acclaimed works and it introduces readers to one of Faulkner's major themes: his ambivalent response to the myth of the Old South, romantic and critical in turn. Also, *The Unvanquished* and *Sartoris* together highlight the tension in Faulkner's career between writing as a source of income versus artistic satisfaction.

Bayard Sartoris II is the narrator and main character of *The Unvanquished*, and the novel is set during and after the Civil War as Bayard matures from a boy of 12 in 1862 to a young man of 24. He and his companion, an African American slave called Ringo, grow into maturity by confronting a war that, from a child's point of view, at first seems glamorous but becomes increasingly grim and tragic. Bayard idealizes his father, Colonel John Sartoris (closely modeled on Faulkner's great-grandfather and namesake, William Clark Falkner). Col. Sartoris embodies for his son the heroic view of war. He commands a unit of partisan cavalry that conducts daring raids on the occupying Union army in northern Mississippi. His actions, however, set in motion a cycle of violence over the course of the novel that Bayard must confront and ultimately transcend.

Sartoris, though written a decade before *The Unvanquished*, is set almost fifty years later in 1919 and thus is a sort of sequel to the later-written novel. Faulkner had hit his stride as a writer by exploring in *Sartoris* his "postage stamp of native soil," the mythical county of Yoknapatawpha. His apprentice fiction in the mid-1920s had been derivative of other writers (such as Sherwood Anderson), but when he began to create his fictional county, he discovered a powerfully unique voice and sense of authority as a writer.

He built his third novel (originally titled *Flags in the Dust*) around Bayard Sartoris II in old age and his grandson, Bayard III. By 1919, the aristocratic Sartoris clan is in decline, and old Bayard finds himself confronting in his grandson the code of foolhardy, destructive behavior inherited from his father. This code is at the heart of the myth of the South that Faulkner both revered and criticized in his work. It set a standard of courage and honor as well as violence and recklessness that haunted the Sartoris family, making them a symbol of the Lost Cause and, in Bayard III, the Lost Generation of World War I. The novel was published in shortened and revised form as *Sartoris* in 1929, and in conjunction with *The Unvanquished*, it provides a strong foundation for approaching Faulkner's body of work.

THE UNVANQUISHED (1938)

Point of View and Setting

Although sometimes considered a loose collection of seven stories, *The Unvanquished* is a highly unified, if episodic, novel narrated by Bayard Sartoris II that traces the stages of his transition into manhood. The language Bayard uses to narrate his story is that of an adult looking back at his youth, but he limits his observations mostly to what his younger self perceives and understands. Occasionally, he notes that he knows better now, as when he describes his father smelling like what "I believed was the smell of powder and glory, the elected victorious but know better now: know

now to have been only the will to endure" (10). It is important to keep in mind that Bayard's initial romanticizing of his father and the war gives way in stages to a more complex, critical view.

The main setting of the novel is the Sartoris plantation in Jefferson, Mississippi, during and after the Civil War, where women, children, and slaves are left alone to endure the invasion of their homeland while marauding Confederates wage guerilla warfare with the occupying Union troops. On the surface of the narrative, Faulkner evokes stereotypes of Southern gallantry in the face of defeat: indomitable matriarchs facing down the Yankees, loyal slaves standing beside their mistresses, fearless soldiers pulling off daring raids. Yet, all of these stereotypes are challenged and complicated in subtle ways.

The social and cultural setting of the novel is governed by rigid traditional expectations of class, gender, and race. The Sartorises, at the top of the social structure, are aristocratic planters who dominate the tradesmen, owners of smaller farms, and slaves on the basis of long-established privilege. In this society, women such as Bayard's Granny Rosa Millard are keepers of the flame of tradition, bound by gender roles that define and constrain them as *ladies* but command respect for their idealized positions. African American slaves, in this worldview, are property without human rights. Faulkner presents this traditional society faithfully—and thus in ways that trouble our contemporary sensibilities, especially in regard to race. Yet his view of this world constantly calls its assumptions into question through plot development and characterization.

Plot Development

The plot of *The Unvanquished* follows episodes in a boy's initiation into maturity. As Cleanth Brooks writes, it is "a novel about growing up—it is the story of an education" (*William Faulkner: The Yoknapatawpha Country* 84). When we meet 12-year-old Bayard in 1862 in the first section, "Ambuscade" (meaning surprise attack), he is clearly still a child, playing war games in the dirt with Ringo. When Bayard's father, Col. John Sartoris, suddenly arrives from fighting in Tennessee, he seems larger than life to his son—or rather someone who does "bigger things than he was" (10). He prepares the household for a Yankee invasion by burying the family silver and then leaves again during the night. This view of the war as an adventure continues a few days later in Bayard's first face-to-face encounter with Yankee soldiers. He and Ringo fire an old musket at them and run home where Bayard's Granny Millard hides them under her wide hoop skirt. The excitement of the war is benignly rendered from Bayard's 12-year-old's point of view.

In the second and third episodes of the novel, "Retreat" and "Raid," Bayard is 13 and the war continues to seem a thrilling game. He and Ringo help Col. Sartoris fool 60 Yankee soldiers into thinking that they are surrounded, and they watch Sartoris make a daring escape when Yankees arrive to capture him. The romantic adventure in "Retreat" ends bleakly, though, when Ringo's uncle tells the Yankees where the family silver is hidden. Bayard, still intent on the glory of war, barely and obliquely mentions that his home is burned down.

In the third section, "Raid," Bayard visits relatives at their Alabama plantation, Hawkhurst, and listens breathlessly to his cousin Drusilla Hawk tell about a railroad chase and about the Yankees' destruction of the railroad; he feels that "this was it" (95), a glimpse of the glory and nobility of war. However, Drusilla's vivid account is succeeded by a nightmarish experience: a crowd of slaves, surging across a bridge toward freedom, sweeps with them into a river the wagon holding Granny, Ringo, and Bayard. This juxtaposition of the glory in Drusilla's tale with the horror of the river crossing marks a change in Bayard's romantic notions that intensifies in the next episodes when Granny Millard is murdered and he avenges her death.

In "Riposte in Tertio" (a fencing term meaning "counterthrust"), Granny Millard mounts a swindling operation as a counterthrust at the Yankees for their having stolen the family silver and mules. She forges letters of requisition for scores of mules, and then she sells the mules to other Yankee regiments to help her poor neighbors. This scheme eventually backfires when a Confederate raider named Grumby shoots Granny Millard. In "Vendée" (the title suggests a vendetta), the fifth section, Bayard and Ringo, now 15, track down Grumby and kill him, cutting off his hand and fastening it to Granny Millard's grave marker as a symbol of their revenge.

The action of the sixth section of the novel, "Skirmish at Sartoris," occurs shortly after the war's end in 1865 during Reconstruction. Col. Sartoris, continuing to live by a code of violence, murders two carpetbaggers from the North who are trying to secure voting rights for blacks. Col. Sartoris is himself murdered in 1873 by a political rival in the last section, "An Odor of Verbena." Expected to avenge his father's death, 24-year-old Bayard chooses to confront his father's killer unarmed, completing his initiation into manhood with the development of a new, nonviolent code of honor.

Characters and Themes

Bayard Sartoris struggles to define himself in relation to the codes and values that he has inherited from his family and environment. He abandons his childishly romantic views of war and becomes a man at 15 when he avenges the death of his grandmother. The tone of the novel changes dramatically in "Vendée" as Bayard makes his transition into manhood, becoming grim and somber to match his outlook. He avenges Granny Millard's murder, not for the sake of a formal code, but out of his personal grief and outrage at Southern scavengers who do not respect women and children—unlike even the occupying Yankees. This act becomes for Bayard the essence of a moral code based not on tradition but personal integrity. In the aftermath of the Civil War, he sees that he can no longer follow the traditions and codes that had previously governed life in the South. In this regard, his cousin Drusilla Hawk is his dramatic foil, a figure who, by contrast, underscores or enhances the traits of a character.

When Bayard visits Drusilla at Hawkhurst in "Raid," she has cut her hair and dresses like a man in defiance of gender norms. She tells Bayard that the war has swept away the conventional life demanded of a Southern woman:

> Living used to be dull, you see. Stupid. You lived in the same house your father was born in . . . and then you grew up and you fell in love with your acceptable young man and in time you would marry him, in your mother's wedding gown perhaps and with the same silver for presents she had received, and then you settled down forever more while your husband got children on your body for you to feed and bathe and dress until they grew up too; and then you and your husband died quietly and were buried together maybe on a summer afternoon just before suppertime. Stupid, you see. But now you can see for yourself how it is, it's fine now; you don't have to worry now about the house and the silver because they get burned up and carried away. (100–01)

In "Skirmish at Sartoris," Bayard tells how he learned that Drusilla had spent the last year of the war fighting beside his father as a fellow soldier. After the war, when her mother discovers that Drusilla is living with Col. Sartoris, she insists that Drusilla stop flouting "all Southern principles of purity and womanhood" (193). Thus, Drusilla is "beaten" and succumbs to wearing dresses and marrying her cousin John Sartoris, in a marriage of convenience. Drusilla, like Bayard, struggles to define for herself a code by which to live that is not constrained by obsolete traditions. Yet, she is ultimately vanquished by the womenfolk who enforce rigidly defined gender roles. Her mother, Rosa Millard's sister, marshals the women of Jefferson to prevail upon Drusilla to mend her unconventional ways. Ironically, in "An Odor of Verbena," Drusilla herself, having been forced to conform to the conventional trappings of Southern womanhood against her will, attempts to enforce a code of violent masculine behavior on Bayard, even making a sexual overture to Bayard to convince him.

In reference to Col. Sartoris's acts of violence and baiting of his political rival Redmond, Drusilla tells Bayard (who is only six years younger than she is) that "There are worse things than killing men, Bayard. There are worse things than being killed. Sometimes I think the finest thing that can happen to a man is to love something, a woman preferably, well, hard hard hard, then to die young because he believed what he could not help but believe and was what he could not (could not? would not) help but be" (227). Drusilla then kisses Bayard, despite his objection that she is his father's wife. Her illicit attraction to Bayard is linked to her advocacy of the masculine code of violence that only he can fulfill. After John Sartoris's murder, Drusilla as stepmother to Bayard ritualistically presents Bayard with dueling pistols, expecting him to take revenge.

Granny Rosa Millard is another strong female character in the novel who finds the war challenging conventional codes of behavior and morality. Her conflict with conventional morality is first introduced in a comic manner, but the comedy turns grim in the course of the novel. With Bayard and Ringo, she enforces strict moral rules: no swearing, no lying, no cheating. Yet, when the Yankees pursue Bayard and Ringo for shooting at them, she hides the boys under her skirt and coolly lies to protect them. Afterward, she is quick to pray for forgiveness, and she washes out the boys' mouths with soap for swearing. Later, when the Yankees burn the Sartoris mansion, she joins the boys in cursing out the Yankees.

Rosa Millard is a rigidly righteous woman, almost a caricature of the feisty indomitable old Southern lady, and Bayard as narrator, in tall-tale fashion, exaggerates the comedy in her quest to get back her property from the Yankees. When she asks for the return of her two stolen mules, named Old Hundred and Tinney, the Yankees misunderstand her and give her 110 mules and a letter of explanation signed by a general. She and Ringo proceed to forge copies of the letter and start a swindling operation, requisitioning mules from one company and selling them to another. Rosa justifies her actions in prayers for forgiveness, adapting her moral code in the context of the war's social disorder. She remains righteous in her pragmatic fashion and adheres to social conventions by dispensing her ill-gotten gains to her poor neighbors, maintaining her aristocratic class standing in a show of noblesse oblige. Ultimately, though, disorder prevails and she is murdered. The farce ends tragically, emphasizing the grimness of Faulkner's comic vision.

Still another character confronting unstable codes is Ringo. More rigid even than the gender and honor codes is the racial code in the Civil War South. Though Ringo lives alongside Bayard and, like him, calls Rosa Millard "Granny," the color line limits him to an unequal, subservient role. His natural talents emerge in the chaos of war, though, and he challenges the racial code. Bayard acknowledges Ringo's superior intelligence. "Father was right; he was smarter than me" (125), he notes, in recounting how Ringo, as Granny Millard's partner in crime, helps to forge documents and keep track of the stolen mules. In contrast to Loosh (who reveals to the Yankees where the silver is buried and runs away for a time), Ringo is loyal to his white master's family. When Col. Sartoris is murdered by Ben Redmond, Bayard notes that Ringo "had outgrown me, had changed so much that summer while he and Granny traded mules with the Yankees that since then I had had to do most of the changing just to catch up with him" (215–16). "Maybe," he adds, "I would never catch up with him" (216). He thought then "that no matter what might happen to either of us, I would never be The Sartoris to him" (215). Ringo proves that the racial code of black inferiority is false even though the disconfirmed code remains in effect.

Even after his death, Col. John Sartoris looms large in *The Unvanquished* and in Faulkner's earlier novel *Sartoris* as The Sartoris, the embodiment of the code of honor that Bayard thinks he will never be to Ringo. The code that Col. Sartoris embodies is associated with the myths of the Old South and the Lost Cause, and Bayard views it and his father with ambivalence. He reveres and loves his father, yet comes to see him (and his intolerance for those who opposed him) clearly and with detachment. When Bayard looks at his dead father, he sees "the eyelids closed over the intolerance" and on his hands "the invisible stain of what had been (once, surely) needless blood" (236).

Bayard recognizes that his father's power became corrupt, leading the Colonel to rash acts of violence such as the murder of the carpet-bagging election workers on his wedding day and of a hill man four years later. Colonel Sartoris's proud intolerance led him to humiliate his former railroad-business partner and later political rival Ben Redmond, until even the Colonel expected Redmond to respond violently. Shortly before their confrontation, Col. Sartoris tells Bayard that, after having acted for years "as the land and the time demanded," it was now time to do "a little moral housecleaning. I am tired of killing men, no matter what the necessity nor the end. Tomorrow when I go to town and meet Ben Redmond, I shall be unarmed" (231–32). So Col. Sartoris, having lived by the sword, dies by it.

His father's violent death leads the community to expect Bayard to avenge it. All the strands of the novel converge as Ringo brings Bayard home from law school after his father's murder. Despite pressure from the community, and especially from Drusilla, for him to kill Redmond, Bayard chooses to face him unarmed and to let him leave town, breaking the cycle of violence at last. Cleanth Brooks interprets this action as transcending, not rejecting, the code.

> Bayard does not resent the community's pressure; he dreads the thought of being dishonored in its eyes. His action, then, is to be thought of not as the rejection of a wrongheaded code of conduct but as the transcendence of that code in a complex action that honors the community's demand that he should call his father's assassin to account, while at the same time acknowledging the higher law embodied in 'Thou shalt not kill.' (*William Faulkner: The Yoknapatawpha Country* 89)

Bayard's transcendence of the code of violence completes his rite of passage into manhood and coalesces the episodic structure of the novel into a unified whole.

SYMBOLS AND ALLUSIONS

A dominant symbol in *The Unvanquished* is the flowering plant verbena (the title of the last chapter of the novel refers to its lemon-scented odor). When Bayard is 20, he walks in the Sartoris garden with Drusilla, who gathers sprigs of verbena to wear in her hair "because she said verbena is the only scent you could smell above the smell of horses and courage" (220). In Greek and Roman cultures, crowns of verbena were worn at weddings and when peace treaties were signed. Winifred Frazer notes "Romans also wore crowns of verbena when challenging an enemy" (Frazer citing William Walker 176). Drusilla puts a sprig of verbena in Bayard's lapel when she ritualistically presents him with dueling pistols to avenge his father's death. After facing his father's killer unarmed, Bayard returns home to learn that Drusilla has gone away, leaving a sprig of verbena on his pillow. For Drusilla verbena is a symbol of violent conflict, but Bayard transforms it to a symbol of peace. By placing verbena on his pillow, she acknowledges Bayard's transcendence of violence. Faulkner described her gesture as "an accolade of optimism," its being alive "a promise of renewal for next year" (Gwynn and Blotner 255–56).

Faulkner elaborates his use of verbena as a symbol with an allusion to Greek tragedy. Bayard describes Drusilla as "the Greek amphora priestess of a succinct and formal violence" (219) when she stands posed with verbena in her hair and her arms outstretched, presenting the dueling pistols to him. The references to a Greek priestess, to the theatricality of Drusilla's appearance, and to the men of the community as a chorus (234) evokes the *Oresteia* of Aeschylus, a trilogy of plays set after the Trojan War in which a cycle of family vengeance is finally ended with mercy for Orestes, who has murdered his mother Clytemnestra in revenge for her murder of Agamemnon, his father. The heightened effect created by the allusion elevates the concluding story's level of artistry, contributing to it being widely recognized as the finest segment of the novel.

Alternative Reading: Feminist Criticism

To read Faulkner from a gender perspective is to look for ways in which society's views of gender shape his characters (both male and female) and how they are represented. A key assumption of such a reading, according to Myra Jehlen, is that "biological sex does not directly or even at all generate the characteristics generally associated with it. Culture, society, history define gender, not nature" (263). Although Faulkner is sometimes criticized for upholding hierarchical patriarchal (even misogynistic) attitudes toward women, gender-based criticism raises questions about the ways in which Faulkner represents women and men and their relative power in society. A particularly rich case study for a gender-based reading is Drusilla Hawk Sartoris in *The Unvanquished*, whose transgressions of gender roles blur the distinction between feminine and masculine roles.

As described above, Drusilla grew up in the antebellum South, subject to the rigid gender code of a Southern belle. She was expected to marry, to have children, and to run a household. The chaos of the war allowed Drusilla to escape the constraints of this code and temporarily to enjoy an androgynous freedom, but when the war was over, she was forced to revert to convention by marrying, wearing skirts, and taking action only indirectly through the influence she exerts over men. Yet, even when she conformed on the surface, she retained a strain of androgyny that both parodies and critiques the conventional gender code.

Her marriage to John Sartoris is not the resolution of a conventional romance. When her mother forces her to wear a dress, Sartoris says to her, "It don't matter. Come. Get up, soldier" (201), addressing her as a comrade in arms rather than a suitor. In narrating the episode, Bayard refers seven times to Drusilla being beaten, and when her mother demands that Sartoris marry her, he also acknowledges, "They have beat you, Drusilla" (203). Thus Drusilla marries him in obedience to him as her commanding officer and to the women of the town as a superior army, inwardly still resisting the gender code by behaving as a soldier fighting a losing battle. Furthermore, Sartoris and Drusilla are not in love with each other. When Drusilla kisses Bayard (as discussed above) and he tells his father about it, Bayard realizes that "it didn't even matter" to Col. Sartoris (231).

Despite succumbing to the conventions of her gender role, Drusilla identifies with men. Explaining to her mother about fighting beside Sartoris, she exclaims "*We* went to the War to hurt Yankees, not hunting women!" (197; emphasis added). When Bayard questions his father's treatment of Redmond, Drusilla argues for the masculine code of honor and violence. After Redmond kills her husband and she realizes that Bayard is not going to avenge the murder, she goes mad. Her identification with masculine codes dictates revenge; the conventions of femininity require that she achieve it through Bayard. When she cannot prevail upon him to do her bidding, the tension is unbearable and she becomes hysterical. In his portrayal of Drusilla's double bind, Faulkner critiques rigid traditional gender roles and demonstrates the debilitation that results when innovative gender roles are stymied in response to changing social conditions.

Faulkner achieves further emphasis on gender in the novel in his portrayals of Granny Rosa Millard and Aunt Jenny Sartoris Du Pre, the sister of Col. Sartoris who only appears in "An Odor of Verbena." Both women are celibate widows who enact the roles of traditional Southern women and thus bring into higher relief Drusilla's conflict with the stultifying rigidity of the norms enforced by her mother and the other ladies of Jefferson. Granny Millard rises to the challenge of running the household during the war, although she eventually is killed when she ventures out of the feminine domestic sphere into the masculine political and military worlds. "She becomes fixed in the feminine sphere once she is murdered," according to Diane Roberts, "a passive, pathetic, victim of a crime that must be avenged by her grandson and his slave Ringo" (17). Aunt Jenny, a young widow, moves in with her brother's family after the war, bringing what Roberts calls "feminine objects—stained glass (with its pietistic suggestion), old sherry, and cuttings of jasmine from the garden" of her ancestral home in Carolina (24). Drusilla's opposite, Miss Jenny supports Bayard in his nonviolent response to the murder of Col. Sartoris; she is "associated not with the astringent smell of martial verbena but the gentler aroma of jasmine" (Roberts, *Faulkner and Southern Womanhood* 25). Miss Jenny lives on with her nephew into old age to be depicted in *Sartoris* as the teller of romantic tales that define the Sartoris men as brave yet reckless, heroic but self-destructive.

SARTORIS (1929)

In writing the stories about Bayard's coming of age that became *The Unvanquished,* Faulkner wanted to make money. A decade earlier when he wrote a novel about the end of Bayard's life, he felt that he had written "THE book" (Blotner, *Selected Letters* 38), a work of art that would establish him as an important writer. To Faulkner's chagrin, the novel, originally titled *Flags in the Dust*, was rejected by the publisher of his first two novels and about ten other publishers before Harcourt, Brace agreed to publish a shortened version of it as *Sartoris*. A flawed, loosely structured novel, still it is extremely important as a transition to Faulkner's major fiction. "Beginning with *Sartoris*," Faulkner stated in an interview, "I discovered that my own little postage stamp of native soil was worth writing about and that I would never live long enough to exhaust it . . . so I created a cosmos of my own" (Meriwether and Millgate 255).

Set in 1919, the novel portrays a generation contemporary with Faulkner himself, drifting in the aftermath of World War I. This so-called Lost Generation includes the novel's protagonist, Bayard Sartoris III, grandson of the Bayard of *The Unvanquished*, another major character. To briefly summarize it, the novel begins with the return home to Jefferson at the war's end of young Bayard, a fighter pilot, grieving over the death of his twin brother Johnny who died in combat by jumping from a burning airplane. Unlike his grandfather Bayard and his Aunt Jenny who embraced life after the Civil War, young Bayard is death-haunted, driving his new automobile so recklessly that he causes his grandfather to have a heart attack and die. Unable to face his family, he runs away and dies flying an unsafe plane, at the novel's end. Faulkner sharply contrasts the two generations, each of which were shaped by wars fifty years apart, with an emphasis on the decline of the Sartoris family in that interval.

Faulkner's next novel also focuses on a family in decline. However, after his disappointment with publishers over *Sartoris*, he decided to write for himself alone. "One day I seemed to shut a door between me and all publishers' addresses and book lists. I said to myself, Now I can write" ("Introduction for *The Sound and the Fury*" 227). What he wrote was *The Sound and the Fury*.

4

The Sound and the Fury (1929)

The Sound and the Fury is Faulkner's masterpiece and his favorite of his books, though he referred to it as his most splendid failure. The disjointed structure of the novel so challenges readers that it can seem formidable. Faulkner deliberately disorients the reader, creating an emotional experience that makes sense only gradually, but the novel richly rewards those who make the effort to piece together the fragments Faulkner provides. There is no substitute for diving into the book, finding one's own way through it, and trusting subsequent readings to clarify meaning. *The Sound and the Fury* is a novel that demands re-reading.

Faulkner explained to students at the University of Virginia in 1957 that *The Sound and the Fury* originated in a vision of a little girl with "muddy drawers" climbing a tree to look through a parlor window. As he considered the image, Faulkner also saw her three brothers

> that didn't have the courage to climb the tree waiting to see what she saw. And I tried first to tell it with one brother, and that wasn't enough. That was Section One. I tried with another brother, and that wasn't enough. That was Section Two. I tried the third brother, because Caddy was still to me too beautiful and too moving to reduce her to telling what was going on, that it would be more passionate to see her through somebody else's eyes, I thought. And that failed and I tried myself—the fourth section—to tell what happened, and I still failed. (Gwynn and Blotner 1)

Occupying the absent center of *The Sound and the Fury*, then, is the little girl with the muddy drawers, Candace Compson, called Caddy, Faulkner's "heart's darling" (Gwynn and Blotner 6). The novel is a series of subjective first-person accounts by each of her three brothers of how she affected them, ending with a relatively objective account by a third-person narrator that focuses on the family's black cook.

In an introduction that Faulkner wrote in 1933 (five years after the novel appeared in 1929) but chose not to publish, he declared that the image of Caddy in the tree and her brothers looking up at her muddy drawers was "perhaps the only thing in literature which would ever move me very much" ("An Introduction" 1972 227). In exploring that image, he discovered that the girl was in the tree to look through a window at her grandmother's funeral and her underwear was muddy because she and her brothers had been playing in a branch (or creek). In another draft of the introduction, Faulkner wrote that the "peaceful glinting of that branch was to become the dark, harsh flowing of time sweeping her to where she could not return . . . , but that just separation, division would not be enough, not far enough. It must sweep her into dishonor and shame too" ("An Introduction" 1973 230).

In this initial tableau that inspired him to write *The Sound and the Fury*, Faulkner found the core theme of the novel: loss. The Compson brothers were to lose Caddy; she would be swept by time from the innocence of childhood into dishonor and shame.

SETTING

Faulkner chose to set each of the novel's four sections on different specific dates—three around Easter in 1928 in Jefferson, Mississippi—but he does not present them in chronological order. In addition, the first two sections emphasize key flashbacks to periods that fill in the Compson family's story. Thus, the first section, narrated by Benjy, the youngest and mentally handicapped sibling, is set on Saturday, April 7, 1928, in Jefferson, and highlights scenes from the early childhood of the Compson children around the turn of the century. The second section, narrated by Quentin, the oldest sibling, is set on June 2, 1910, at Harvard University in Cambridge, Massachusetts, and places emphasis on scenes from 1909 and earlier in 1910. The third section, narrated by Jason, the third sibling, is set on Friday, April 6, 1928 in Jefferson, the day before Benjy's section. The final section, narrated by a third-person narrator, occurs on Easter Sunday, April 8, 1928, and follows Dilsey Gibson, the Compson cook, as she prepares meals and takes Benjy with her to church.

The Sound and the Fury is set in Yoknapatawpha County, and it builds on the fictional cosmos that Faulkner explored in *Sartoris*. The Compsons, another of the first families of Jefferson, have a distinguished lineage that includes a state governor and generals. Although their fortunes have declined, the Compson house, the remnant of a once-grand estate, is a reminder of the Compsons' place in the county's history. *The Sound and the Fury* is focused more inwardly, however, on the claustrophobic dynamics of a single family, in comparison to other Yoknapatawpha novels. As the novel progresses, the focus broadens to present more of the social world of Jefferson. In section 3, Jason is very concerned with his family's reputation in the town. He objects when Caddy, after their father's funeral, makes a scene at the store where he works and insists that she meet him in a less public place. He also berates his niece Quentin in 1928 for flaunting the middle-class values of the town with her truancy and promiscuity. Jason aspires to the crass, business-oriented new South that, at the time the novel is set, was supplanting the old agrarian South that had been dominated by long-established aristocratic families. Mrs. Compson proudly identifies Jason with her family's lower-class Bascomb line more than the Compson line into which she married and to which she felt socially inferior.

Section 4 of the novel expands the setting somewhat to include Dilsey Gibson's black church community in which she enjoys the status of being attached to so-called quality white folks. Through Dilsey's family, *The Sound and the Fury* includes another layer of Yoknapatawpha society, but the novel shows the Gibsons mostly in their relation to the Compsons.

Faulkner provides further information about the setting of the novel in sources external to it. In 1945 Faulkner wrote an appendix to the novel as an introduction to an excerpt published in 1946 in *The Portable Faulkner,* edited by Malcolm Cowley. Some editions of the novel include the appendix, but Noel Polk argues that it is essentially a separate although related text, like Faulkner's 1936 novel *Absalom, Absalom!* in which Quentin and his father are major characters (see chapter 7) and short stories such as "That Evening Sun" about the Compsons (see chapter 8) (Polk 12–13).

PLOT AND STRUCTURE

Theorists of narrative distinguish between story (events in their chronological order) and discourse (how these are presented by a writer, "especially changes of time sequence, the presentation of the consciousness of the characters, and the narrator's relation to the story and the audience") (Martin 108). In analyzing the plot and structure of *The Sound and the Fury,* this distinction is helpful. Thus, I will discuss the plot and structure of *The Sound and the Fury* in terms of its story. In discussing the characters, I will look at the discourse of the narrators—that is, how their respective points of view filter and shape the stories they tell.

Critics have examined *The Sound and the Fury* carefully to determine the chronology of the events of the novel, noting that Faulkner often provides clues to the frequent and abrupt time shifts in the first two sections. In their glossary and commentary on the book, *Reading Faulkner: The Sound and the Fury*, Stephen Ross and Noel Polk provide a useful summary of the novel's chronology (citing their evidence from the novel and from Faulkner's comments on it). They determine that Quentin, Caddy, Jason, and Benjy were born in 1890, 1892, 1894, and 1895, respectively, and that the sight of Caddy's muddy drawers—the inciting event of the novel as discussed above—occurred in 1900 at the time of the funeral of the children's grandmother (called Damuddy).

Both Benjy and Quentin are strongly affected by Caddy's burgeoning sexuality. In 1906, Benjy, who associates the smell of trees with Caddy, becomes upset when she puts on perfume to attract boys and only calms down when she washes it off. When she loses her virginity, he also senses it, crying and insisting she wash off her changed scent. The oldest brother, Quentin, views his sister's virginity as a symbol of the family's honor and picks an ineffectual fight with her lover Dalton Ames. Quentin's puritanical obsession with Caddy's virginity leads him paradoxically to imagine an incestuous relationship with her so that they would be alone together in hell for all time.

When Caddy becomes pregnant, a hasty marriage is arranged to Herbert Head (who does not know that she is pregnant with another man's child) in April 1910. Quentin, in despair, drowns himself several months later at the end of his first year in college at Harvard. Caddy's husband divorces her soon after their wedding, and, in disgrace, she leaves her daughter (named Quentin for her dead brother) with her parents and disappears. Caddy's loss haunts Benjy, who cries whenever he is reminded of her—even when golfers on the course near the house call for a caddie. The land for the golf course had been owned by the Compsons and known as Benjy's Pasture. It had been sold to pay for Caddy's wedding and for Quentin's Harvard education, a sign of the family's decline, accelerated by the death of Mr. Compson from alcoholism in 1912. Jason, who as a child is a stingy tattletale, becomes increasingly embittered by the family's circumstances and cheats his niece Quentin out of the money that Caddy has sent for child support. Jason's cruelty drives Quentin to steal the hoarded money and run away with a carnival worker at Easter in 1928.

This summary account of the story behind the discourse of the novel does not begin to account for its richness and complexity, but it provides a framework for discussion of the novel's characters and themes.

CHARACTERS

Benjy

The title of *The Sound and the Fury* alludes to a line spoken by Shakespeare's Macbeth when he hears of the death of Lady Macbeth: "Life's but a walking shadow, . . . a tale / Told by an idiot, full of sound and fury, / Signifying nothing" (*Macbeth* V:v, lines 26–30). Faulkner begins his novel as a tale told by a literal idiot by placing the reader initially inside the consciousness of the mentally handicapped Benjy, whose mind records his experiences and memories without understanding their significance. Faulkner, however, provides careful readers with clues that make it possible for them to understand Benjy's internal monologue, even if he cannot.

First, Faulkner gives the date of Benjy's monologue as April 7, 1928, which we soon learn is Benjy's thirty-third birthday. Whenever something reminds Benjy of the past, his narration jumps to that past moment. With little understanding of time, Benjy narrates his memories of the past as if they are happening in the present. Faulkner often signals these transitions with a change of typeface (into or out of italics) and with references (to weather or to Benjy's caretakers) that mark specific episodes. Paying attention to such clues orients the reader to the time shifts in Benjy's section. For example, Benjy's caretaker in April 1928 is Dilsey's teenage grandson Luster. Benjy's narration first slips into the past when he gets snagged on a nail while crawling through a fence. In the next passage, in italics, Caddy unsnags him and mentions how cold it is and that Christmas is coming in two days. Then, in the next paragraph, in roman type to signal that the time has changed again (to only a short while before Caddy unsnagged him), Benjy's caretaker is Versh, Luster's uncle. Eventually we learn that the date is December 23, 1908, when Benjy is 13 years old. Versh looks after Benjy during his childhood, another son of Dilsey's named T. P. in his later teen years, and Luster after that.

Ross and Polk identify 14 distinct time levels in Benjy's section. The recurring motif dominating them all is the presence or absence of Caddy and of objects associated with her. When present, Caddy nurtures and protects Benjy, acting as a surrogate mother. Mrs. Compson, a neurotically self-absorbed hypochondriac, withholds love from all her children, creating a vacuum that, in various ways, all of her brothers turn to Caddy to fill. Benjy's most poignant memories involve stages in Caddy's sexual maturation and resulting disappearance from his life. In 1900, her muddy drawers foreshadow the loss of innocence that eventually sweeps her away. In 1906, her use of perfume masks the innocent scent of trees that he associates with her. In 1908 or 1909, he senses and mourns her lost virginity. In 1910, her wedding signals her departure (Bleikasten, *Ink of Melancholy* 62–63). Benjy constantly oscillates between comfort and pain. Sources of comfort for him are Caddy herself and, when she is gone, such reminders of her as her slipper or the warmth of fire. The absence of Caddy or her substitutes provokes bellowing and tears in Benjy, who in his nonverbal anguish embodies the pain of loss.

The losses that Benjy endures include a series of deaths as well as the loss of Caddy. He looks up at Caddy's muddy drawers with his brothers as she looks in at their grandmother's funeral. Benjy's memories juxtapose Damuddy's death with memories of the deaths of Quentin in 1910 and Mr. Compson in 1912. Shortly after Caddy has married and left home, 15-year-old Benjy waits for her at the gate, expecting her to return. One day, the gate is left unlocked and he frightens some schoolgirls. As a result, he is castrated, the death of sex for him. Benjy also experiences a loss of identity. When it becomes apparent that he is mentally handicapped, Mrs. Compson changes his name from Maury (after her brother) to Benjamin, Joseph's brother in the biblical book of Genesis.

Quentin

In his hyperarticulate way, Quentin is also obsessed with the loss of Caddy and her lost innocence and, even more, with death. Although Benjy's section is disorienting, there is a logic to it that is ultimately less obscure than Quentin's tortured and highly allusive stream of consciousness. As in Benjy's section, though, there is a specific time and place in which Quentin's monologue occurs and there are some clearly distinguishable flashbacks, some of which retell episodes from Benjy's section from Quentin's perspective.

Quentin's monologue takes place on the day of his suicide, June 2, 1910, at the end of his first year at Harvard. Over the course of the day, he prepares for his death by making various fastidious arrangements. These include buying a pair of flatirons to weight him down under water and depositing them under the bridge near Harvard where he plans to drown himself. He rides streetcars through the Boston and Cambridge environs, and befriends a little lost Italian girl whom he calls sister. When he tries to help the girl find her way home, her brother accuses him of trying to abduct her, and a justice of the peace fines Quentin. Quentin's roommate and two other classmates find him and take him on a picnic where he gets into a fight. Returning to his dormitory room, he bathes and changes clothes in preparation for his suicide.

Throughout the day, Quentin obsesses about Caddy. He remembers childish sexual play that he engaged in with a girl named Natalie that caused a fight between him and his sister; he also recalls Caddy's involvement with several boys, especially Dalton Ames, to whom she presumably lost her virginity. His memories also include the days leading up to Caddy's marriage to Herbert Head.

In his monologue, Quentin alludes to a fantasy of incest with Caddy. He even confesses to their father that he has committed incest with Caddy, although Faulkner stated later that Quentin fantasized his confession also (Gwynn and Blotner 262–63). Quentin's obsession with his sister's sexuality reveals his own anxieties about sex. Although he tells Caddy he has "done that" (151), he is almost certainly sexually inexperienced. He wants to stop time and preserve a static, unchanging state of innocence with Caddy. Realizing the futility of that wish, he embraces death as the ultimate stasis.

Quentin's language is rich with images of time. At the beginning of his last day, he breaks the hands off his pocket watch and avoids clocks; he is highly aware of the position of his shadow as a symbol of time passing. According to Edmond L. Volpe, "Quentin, in effect, kills himself to stop time because time is the ultimate reality" (*A Reader's Guide to William Faulkner: The Novels* 115) and Quentin cannot cope with reality. Though he thinks of himself as an idealist, holding to a static tradition of southern gentility and female purity, his self-absorption makes his idealism more of a façade. Furthermore, present reality for Quentin is a fluid refutation of that static image of an ideal past.

Quentin reveals his allegiance to southern gentility in his interaction with other southerners at Harvard. One of them is an elderly black man called Deacon who flatters students from the South by enacting the role of a servile Negro, even as Deacon subverts the social conventions that govern southern race relations, such as calling Quentin "boy." Quentin makes a point to leave Deacon his best suit because he reminds Quentin of Dilsey's husband, Roskus, and of the nurture and serenity they provided him growing up. Other southerners are the Kentuckians Gerald Bland, a fellow student, and his pretentious mother. "To Quentin," according to Volpe, "the Blands represent a deterioration of Southern society, but despite his contempt for them, Quentin is drawn into their company, because they represent, however burlesqued, the traditional world he considers his heritage" (107–08). Ironically, their superficiality and bigotry are probably closer to the reality of plantation aristocracy than Quentin's idealized concept of it, Volpe notes.

Quentin yearns for an ideal world of innocence, gentility, and chivalry without change. He makes Caddy the focus of this unreal world and cannot accept losing her as she matures sexually. Assuming a chivalrous role, he tries to fend off her suitors but fails. The climactic scene of his section occurs on a picnic with the Blands, when Gerald's boasting of his success with women triggers Quentin's extended memory of Caddy's sexual involvement with Dalton Ames, including Quentin's ineffectual showdown with Ames. In Quentin's memory (the reliability of which is unclear), he orders Ames to leave town. When Ames says that some fellow or other was bound to have sex with Caddy, Quentin asks "did you ever have a sister did you." He replies "no but theyre [sic] all bitches," and Quentin slaps him. In the fight that ensues, Quentin faints, failing completely in his chivalrous quest to protect Caddy.

On the picnic, Quentin, as if in a trance, suddenly blurts out to Gerald Bland the question, "Did you ever have a sister? Did you?" and hits him, a doubling of the (remembered? imagined?) scene with Ames. Bland, like Ames, easily overpowers Quentin, bloodying his face. After the fight, at dusk, Quentin returns to his dorm room to change clothes and make his final ritualistic preparations for his suicide.

Jason

In the third section of the novel, the last Compson brother, Jason, speaks on the Friday before Easter 1928, the day before Benjy's section is set. Like his brothers, Jason is also obsessed with Caddy, although he mediates his obsession through her daughter Quentin. Caddy's marriage to Herbert Head was supposed to lead to a well-paying bank job for Jason, but when the marriage collapsed, so did Jason's job prospects. For years he vented his resentment over the lost opportunity by stealing the money that Caddy periodically sent for her daughter's support.

Jason's monologue is a furious rant that famously begins "Once a bitch always a bitch, what I say," referring to his niece. For good reason, Faulkner called Jason the "most vicious character in my opinion I ever thought of" (Meriwether and Millgate 146). His undisguised misogyny and bigotry combine with his paranoia to make his hatefulness a vivid source of grotesquely dark comedy after the poetic romanticism of Quentin's monologue.

Jason's cynicism about his family presents the Compsons in the grotesque mode known as southern gothic, as André Bleikasten points out:

> Described without nuance, stripped of everything that might earn them understanding or pity, the protagonists of the family drama now become the typecast actors of a burlesque Southern melodrama halfway between [Erskine] Caldwell and Tennessee Williams: alcoholics for a father and an uncle, a whining hypochondriac for a mother, a shameless trollop for a niece, and a drooling idiot for a brother, such are the *dramatis personae* in section 3. Small wonder that the tale of their mishaps, including Jason's own, turns to Gothic farce. (*Ink of Melancholy* 107)

Jason's contrasting view of the Compsons, however, still shares important characteristics with those of Benjy and Quentin. In his own way, Jason is as impotent as Benjy and as obsessed with female chastity as Quentin.

Jason spends the day of his monologue in furious activity that leads to nothing. He speculates in the stock market only to lose money, and he rushes around after his niece and the carnival pitchman to no avail. Although sharing none of his brother Quentin's prudishness about sex, Jason is obsessively concerned with his niece's promiscuity. These elements provide a sense of repetitive continuity underneath the shocking shift of tone that Jason's section gives the novel.

Jason's obsession with Caddy and her daughter manifests itself in monetary terms. For Jason, Caddy's loss was a loss of money, rather than a loss of love as it was for Benjy or of honor as it was for Quentin. Jason measures the value of people and relationships in financial terms. As a child, he kept his hands in his pockets, and in adulthood he tries to keep his hands on his strongbox—both images of a grasping stinginess. He even keeps his sexual relationship with his girlfriend Lorraine, a prostitute, on a cash basis. In his lack of humanistic values, Jason represents modern alienated man, cut off from any meaningful connection to the past or humankind. Although not a tale told by an idiot, his monologue is indeed full of sound and fury, signifying nothing.

Dilsey

The final section of the novel is a relatively objective, third-person account of Easter Sunday 1928 that mostly follows the Compsons' black cook, Dilsey Gibson, as she prepares breakfast for the family (during which Quentin's escape is discovered) and takes Benjy to her church for Easter services. Section 4 only veers from Dilsey's point of view to narrate an account of Jason's futile pursuit of Quentin after he realizes that she has robbed him. The final passages return to Dilsey and Benjy.

Dilsey is a character of great dignity and integrity despite her humble station. She remains loyal to the Compson family throughout their tribulations, providing much-needed stability and nurture. Unlike the Compsons, she lives a life of service and usefulness, accomplishing the many tasks required to keep the household running. Although she speaks sharply to Jason and Luster and even to Mrs. Compson at times, she treats Benjy and Caddy's daughter with tender protectiveness. She provides an ethical center to the novel through her ability to cope with vicissitudes and her long-suffering endurance.

Olga Vickery notes that "Dilsey's participation in the Easter service is the one meaningful ritual in the book" (49). Preaching the Easter sermon at Dilsey's Baptist Church is a guest preacher, the Rev. Shegog. His colloquial account of Jesus' suffering on the cross and resurrection unites the congregation to where "their hearts were speaking to one another in chanting measures beyond the need for words" (*Sound and the Fury* 294). Benjy sits calm and enrapt beside Dilsey, who cries "rigidly and quietly in the annealment and the blood of the remembered Lamb" (297). Walking home from church, Dilsey continues to weep, saying "I've seed de first en de last" (297). When her daughter asks what she means, "'Never you mind,' Dilsey said. "I seed de beginning, en now I sees de endin'" (297). John T. Matthews insightfully notes that, though Dilsey finds meaning in the Easter service, she cannot or will not explain it, even to her daughter. Rather, "the solitude of the individual outlook reasserts itself; because Dilsey's summing up remains hers alone, we return to a world that lacks social and family unity" (85).

THEMES

In addition to the theme of loss discussed in the context of the focal characters in each section, *The Sound and the Fury* addresses themes related to its fragmented structure as well as to gender and race. The fourth section moves the novel toward a sense of closure in Dilsey's claim to see "de endin." However, Faulkner's modernist vision resists coherence, and he ends the novel with a poignant reminder of Benjy's isolation. To soothe him, Dilsey lets Luster take Benjy on his ritual carriage ride to the cemetery. When Luster varies the routine by turning a different direction around the town square, Benjy begins to bellow. Jason, enraged that Benjy is making a spectacle of himself in public, rushes up and turns the carriage around. Comforted by the restoration of his familiar route, Benjy becomes serene. The sense of community that Dilsey experienced during Shegog's sermon subsides, and we are left with a vision of Benjy alone in his rigid inner world.

The self-enclosed, fragmentary quality of the three monologues that precede the final section suggest a major theme of the novel that is related to its form: the gap between truth and each person's version of it. Michael Millgate explains that "*The Sound and the Fury* is in part concerned with the elusiveness, the multivalence, of truth, or at least with man's persistent and perhaps necessary tendency to make of truth a personal thing: each man, apprehending some fragment of the truth, seizes upon that fragment as though it were the whole truth and elaborates it into a total vision of the world, rigidly exclusive and hence utterly fallacious" (*Achievement* 87). Each brother builds his personal, fragmentary vision of Caddy into a truth that is partial and that isolates him from the social world.

The truth of Caddy herself remains elusive and voiceless in the novel. Faulkner explained that she was "too beautiful and too moving to reduce her to telling what was going on" (Gwynn and Blotner 1). Caddy's elusiveness, her inconsistency as a character (according to feminist critic Dawn Trouard), is essential to the novel's theme of the gap between truth and its perception. Yet her gender suggests that she embodies another theme, the limited role of women in society.

In childhood, Caddy is the natural leader of her brothers; she is brave, loving, and headstrong. As a young woman, she acknowledges her desire for Dalton Ames and rebels against the limits placed on her sexuality until she becomes trapped by her pregnancy and failed marriage. In the third section, Jason shows her defeated, begging and pleading with him to take care of her daughter. "It is hard to see the Caddy of the branch or the Caddy who has survived Dalton, or even the Caddy who has finessed a marriage to an eligible bachelor in this slinking and defeated Caddy" (Trouard 45). This pathetic figure, as much as her brother Quentin's immobilizing idealization of her, is a victim of the limited scope patriarchy allows women.

Caddy's plight is echoed in that of her mother and daughter as well. Mrs. Compson has been reduced by her acceptance of the role of Southern lady to a complaining hypochondriac. Caddy's daughter is literally locked in her room until she escapes—by climbing down the same pear tree that her mother had climbed up to face the reality of the death of her grandmother. In *The Sound and the Fury*, the Compson women are voiceless in contrast to the Compson men, but their unruliness and even oppression indict the patriarchal system that constrains them.

The Compson women are supported and nurtured by Dilsey Gibson, a woman who is marginalized by her race as well as by her gender. Faulkner's treatment of racial marginalization constitutes another theme in the novel. Dilsey is also denied a voice in the novel's narrative scheme, even though the fourth section of the novel is often referred to as Dilsey's section. However, Faulkner deliberately chose to render "her" section in the voice of a seemingly objective third-person narrator who yet maintains a distance from Dilsey's race, such as in a reference to "the rich and unmistakable smell of negroes" (291). This narrator's obvious sympathy toward Dilsey is still marked by a tacit recognition of her as Other. "The narrator cannot help but speak from the position of a literate white southern male," John Matthews notes ("*Sound and the Fury*" 86).

Faulkner's treatment of race in his fiction is controversial. In *The Sound and the Fury,* he does not shrink from presenting racist attitudes, such as Quentin's paternalism and Jason's vitriolic disdain for blacks. The novel contains many uses of the word "nigger" by white as well as by black characters that reflect a usage much more accepted and common at the time and place when the novel is set. However, the novel does at least interrogate the racism in the term when Quentin reflects that "a nigger is not a person so much as a form of behavior; a sort of obverse reflection of the white people he lives among" (86) and thus in the (white) eye of the beholder. When Dilsey uses the term, then, it is an indication of how she has internalized dominant white views of race. On balance, Faulkner presents white and black people relating to one another in complex ways that resist labels such as racist, but the ways in which race divides as well as connects people is a prominent theme in the novel.

SYMBOLS

Because of his poetic sensibility, Quentin's section of *The Sound and the Fury* is particularly rich with symbols. Faulkner reinforces the theme of loss of innocence in Quentin's section through the use of honeysuckle as a symbol of sex. When Quentin realizes that Caddy has lost her virginity, he follows her to the branch where she lies half submerged on the bank. Quentin finds the smell of honeysuckle overwhelming: "the air seemed to drizzle with honeysuckle" (150); "it had got into my breathing it was on her face and throat like paint . . . and I had to pant to get any air at all out of that thick gray honeysuckle" (151). The odor of honeysuckle is inescapable and Quentin connects it to the inevitable loss of innocence that threatens to sweep away his childhood closeness with Caddy (Volpe, *A Reader's Guide to William Faulkner: The Novels* 112).

The grayness that Quentin perceives in the scent of honeysuckle indicates another important symbol in the novel: twilight. Faulkner's original title for the novel was "Twilight," and in such important moments as the "muddy drawers" and the branch scenes, Quentin especially calls attention to the light at dusk, that ambiguous threshold between day and night. Liminality is a term for the threshold condition of being "betwixt and between," and twilight is a powerful symbol of how Quentin is stuck in the liminal transition between innocence and sexual maturity.

Mud and water are also prevalent symbols in Quentin's section. When Caddy interrupts Quentin's childhood sex play with Natalie—whom Caddy calls a "dirty girl" (134)—he muddies himself in a stinking hog-wallow in an act symbolizing his disgust with sexual impurity. When Caddy says that she doesn't care what he was doing, he smears her with mud as well. They purify themselves by washing in the branch, an action repeated when Caddy has lost her virginity. Mud also prefigures sexual impurity in the key scene when Caddy climbs the tree to look in at her grandmother's funeral and her brothers look up at her muddied underwear. Yet another echo of this symbolism occurs in Quentin's description of the little Italian girl he befriends on his last day. Quentin repeatedly emphasizes her dirtiness, which is linked to Caddy by his references to the girl as "sister" and to the irony that he is falsely accused of molesting her in an echo of his false confession of incest with Caddy.

ALTERNATIVE READING: RHETORICAL CRITICISM

In its broadest sense, rhetorical criticism examines how writers communicate with their readers. A rhetorical critic of fiction looks at the strategies and methods that authors use to shape readers' attitudes toward the world of the text and the characters. Basic questions in rhetorical criticism include: Who is the speaker *of* the text, and who are the speakers *in* the text? In the case of fiction, the author is the fundamental speaker *of* the text, but Wayne Booth in *The Rhetoric of Fiction* warns that this speaker is never the historical author but rather an "implied author," a version of the author implied by the text. The "real" author creates this implied version of himself—or herself—by using the language of the text as a kind of screen. From the language of the text, readers infer a set of norms and values that guide their attitudes toward the characters and events of the work.

In his talks to students at the University of Virginia in 1957, Faulkner confused the issue somewhat by referring to the speaker of the fourth section of *The Sound and the Fury* as "Faulkner," as if the real author can speak directly in a novel. He claimed that each of the first three attempts to tell the story "wasn't right" and that when he tried to let Faulkner do it, "that was still wrong" (Gwynn and Blotner 32). In effect, "Faulkner" as the narrator of the fourth section is no more authoritative—just more transparent—than Benjy, Quentin, or Jason as the clearly biased narrators of section 4. All four speakers are only more or less opaque screens for communicating the values of the implied author.

What "Faulkner" as the fourth narrator does offer is a different set of rhetorical strategies. The first three narrators provide vivid but highly subjective accounts of the story. The fourth narrator takes a wider view that encompasses how the Compsons look to an outside observer. We learn, for example, that Benjy's eyes are cornflower blue and that Jason has brown hair "curled into two stubborn hooks, one on either side of his forehead like a bartender in caricature" (279). This more objective view of the world of the novel puts the obsessively skewed perspectives of the previous narrators in context. This narrator, however, is not a mere camera-eye recorder but a speaker who interprets Benjy's bellowing in universal terms as "the grave hopeless sound of all voiceless misery under the sun" (316).

Despite such universalizing statements, John T. Matthews observes that the final narrator "remains outside some of the characters and experiences he would describe. The last section tensely opposes 'Faulkner's' narration and Dilsey's point of view" ("*Sound and the Fury*" 79). This opposition results in the racial generalizations discussed above that reveal the narrator's white perspective on a racialized Other. The blind spots and limitations of even this privileged voice reinforce the themes of the fragmentation of reality and the gap between the seer and the seen that connect the novel's story and its discourse. It is a theme that Faulkner takes up again in *As I Lay Dying*.

5

As I Lay Dying (1930)

William Faulkner claimed that the concept for *As I Lay Dying,* his fifth novel, consisted of taking a family and subjecting them to the twin catastrophes of flood and fire, and that it came to him all at once. He called the novel a simple tour de force, which he explained as the result of technique charging in and taking command of the writer's vision. With such a book "the finished work is simply a matter of fitting bricks neatly together, since the writer knows probably every single word right to the end before he puts the first one down. This happened with *As I Lay Dying.* It was not easy. No honest work is. It was simple in that all the material was already at hand" (Meriwether and Millgate 244). Tour de force further implies dazzling virtuosity of technique. André Bleikasten writes, "Of all Faulkner's novels, [*As I Lay Dying*] is perhaps the most agile, the most adroit, the one in which the writer's new-won mastery of his craft and the versatility of his gifts reveal themselves in the most spectacular ways" (*Ink of Melancholy* 151).

Faulkner wrote *As I Lay Dying* in six weeks starting on October 25, 1929, just a few weeks after *The Sound and the Fury* was published and a few days before the stock market crash that signaled the beginning of the Great Depression. *As I Lay Dying* shares a similar structure with *The Sound and the Fury*: multiple first-person narrators within the same family. However, in *As I Lay Dying* there are monologues by seven family members and they are divided into short alternating sections, as opposed to four long sequential ones, making the work read almost like a play, with speeches identified by the speakers' names. Instead of the three narrating Compson brothers of the earlier novel, there are the four Bundren brothers and their sister and parents in *As I Lay Dying*. Unlike *The Sound and the Fury* with its concluding third-person section, *As I Lay Dying* includes an intermittent chorus of eight neighbors and townspeople who provide glimpses of the Bundrens as they appear to those outside the family. All told, *As I Lay Dying* consists of 59 monologues of varying lengths.

SETTING

As I Lay Dying is Faulkner's third Yoknapatawpha novel. Where *Sartoris* and *The Sound and the Fury* focus on the fictional county's aristocrats, *As I Lay Dying* shifts attention to struggling farmers who work the land around the county seat of Jefferson. Warwick Wadlington observes that *As I Lay Dying* is the last major American novel written in the 1920s and the first one published in the 1930s, and that it thus signals the transition into the national upheaval of the Depression. He notes, though, that the South had not shared the prosperity that the Roaring Twenties brought most of the country. The Bundrens in effect foreshadow the plight of John Steinbeck's Joad family in *The Grapes of Wrath* (1939), another novel of a poor family's journey (*"As I Lay Dying": Stories out of Stories* 4).

In the background of the novel, Wadlington finds a concern with collective action in the face of economic deprivation. Like the country at large during the Depression, the Bundren family must work together for a common goal in spite of their individual problems. Similarly, the townspeople feel obliged to help the Bundrens in their time of need. Unlike in the liberal North, collectivism in the South was associated with conservative populist political campaigns such as the "revolt of the rednecks," named for politician Theodore Bilbo's red ties. The youngest Bundren's name, Vardaman, alludes to the so-called redneck (and blatantly racist) Mississippi senator James K. Vardaman, who campaigned with Bilbo. According to Wadlington, "Faulkner's family had participated energetically, though ambivalently, in these politics" (*"As I Lay Dying": Stories out of Stories* 7).

PLOT AND STRUCTURE

As I Lay Dying has a simple basic plot structure—that of an epic journey—yet Faulkner overlays it with a complex mix of tragic and grotesquely funny elements. The purpose of the Bundren family's journey is to fulfill Anse Bundren's promise to bury his wife Addie with her family in Jefferson. The major obstacles to the journey are trials by flood and fire: a flooded river that they must cross in their wagon and the burning of a barn where Addie's coffin is sheltered overnight. The action of the novel is compressed into 10 days, beginning with the day of Addie's death and concluding the day after her burial, but occasional flashbacks fill in important episodes in the past.

As in *The Sound and the Fury*, Faulkner withholds key information, forcing the reader to construct the story of the Bundren family from the fragmentary discourse of the various narrators' monologues. The withheld information includes several secrets that characters try to keep hidden, and we as readers participate in the family dynamic of secrecy, struggling to understand what is being kept from us. Eventually we learn that Addie's disappointment with her husband Anse Bundren led her, after giving Anse two sons (Cash and Darl), to have an adulterous affair with Reverend Whitfield, producing her third son Jewel. After the affair ended, she had two more children with Anse, a daughter (Dewey Dell) and a fourth son (Vardaman). She made Anse promise to bury her in Jefferson, which was a several days' journey from their home. At the time the novel begins, Cash and Darl are probably in their late twenties, Jewel about eighteen, Dewey Dell seventeen, and Vardaman a child of seven or eight. Cash, a carpenter, makes Addie's coffin as she lies dying, and after her death the family carries Addie's body by wagon to Jefferson. Each member of the family hides a private obsession or a selfish reason for wanting to go to Jefferson in addition to burying Addie: Anse wants to get a set of false teeth, Cash would like to buy a graphophone, Dewey Dell needs to get an abortion, and Vardaman covets a toy train. Jewel, his mother's favorite, is single-mindedly focused on accomplishing the task of getting her buried, and Darl is obsessed to the point of insanity with jealousy of Jewel as their mother's favorite child.

Compounding Darl's instability is his acute awareness of the grotesque absurdity of their disaster-prone mission to bury Addie. Vardaman, not understanding death, thinks Addie can't breathe in the coffin and bores holes in it that disfigure her corpse. As the family fords a flooded river, the wagon and the coffin are swept away. Jewel heroically rescues the coffin, but Cash breaks his leg and the mules drown. Anse sells Jewel's prized horse to replace the mules and the journey continues as the decaying corpse begins to smell, attracting buzzards and the dismayed disgust of people on the road.

Finally, to end the outrageous journey, Darl sets a fire in a barn where Addie's coffin is placed overnight, and again Jewel rescues the coffin. After the burial, the family commits Darl to an insane asylum. In a final absurd turn of events, Anse marries the woman from whom he borrowed the spades to bury Addie and the novel ends as he introduces her to his children by saying "Meet Mrs Bundren."

The Bundrens' journey and its tribulations link the novel structurally and generically to such epics as Homer's *Odyssey* (the title is an allusion to that work which will be discussed later). Yet, epic tales traditionally present heroic figures engaging in adventures and great achievements. The Bundrens are far from heroic adventurers, although they display remarkable courage and stoicism. Their low social status and selfish obsessions turn their journey into more of a mock epic and leaven their family tragedy with gallows humor. Faulkner once noted that "there's not too fine a distinction between humor and tragedy, that even tragedy is in a way walking a tightrope between the ridiculous—between the bizarre and the terrible" (Gwynn and Blotner 39). Faulkner's mixture of bizarre humor and terrible tragedy give *As I Lay Dying* its uniquely mixed qualities and tone.

CHARACTERS

Darl

Darl is the first narrator we encounter in *As I Lay Dying*. He speaks 19 of the novel's 59 sections—almost one-third—and the frequency of his monologues is such that we never leave his consciousness for long. No more than four other voices ever speak in a row before Darl takes over again. His voice is also privileged with a limited omniscience that is denied the other characters. He occasionally narrates scenes at which he is not present, such as Addie's death; at other times he communicates telepathically (primarily with Dewey Dell) or clairvoyantly knows his family's secrets, such as Dewey Dell's pregnancy and Jewel's parentage.

Darl is thus highly sensitive to other members of his family, and his use of language further reveals the heightened sensibility of a poet and artist. Watson Branch connects this sensibility in Darl in part to his exposure in France during World War I to cubist art. In Darl's last section, while raving on the train taking him to the asylum in Jackson, Darl refers to himself in the third person: "Darl had a little spy-glass he got in France at the war" (254), establishing that Darl served as a soldier in France. During the fire in the Gillespie barn, Darl describes Addie's coffin on the sawhorses as looking "like a cubistic bug" (219). Branch deduces that Darl's allusion to cubism reveals a familiarity with the art of Paul Cezanne, Pablo Picasso, and other cubists who presented multiple views of subjects simultaneously in their paintings. More profoundly, Branch argues, Darl's experiences with cubism in France during the war gave him a new way of seeing reality, "reality as it is conceived by the mind, the senses operating in conjunction with the memory and imagination, rather than as it is perceived by the eye, from one fixed viewpoint at one instant in time" (118). In this way, Darl echoes Faulkner's own experiences seeing cubist art in France in 1925 (Blotner, *Faulkner* 160).

Along with his hypersensitivity and artistic sensibility, Darl also struggles with identity and a weak sense of self. In one remarkable passage, Darl states flatly "I don't know what I am. I don't know if I am or not" (80). He contrasts himself with Jewel, a man of action who does not question his existence. A psychological explanation would be that Addie shut Darl out from the love she lavished on Jewel, and this lack of mothering weakened Darl's sense of self. In compensation, he intrudes obsessively into the hidden lives of his family, learning their secrets intuitively. Darl's compensatory obsessiveness ultimately provokes his downfall, though. When he defies Jewel by trying to put an end to the grotesque treatment of Addie's body that the journey to Jefferson entails, he breaks the law by burning the Gillespie barn, and his family commits him to a mental institution. In his final monologue, on the train to the asylum in Jackson, he is reduced to hysterical laughter.

Addie

Although Addie speaks only one of the novel's monologues, she dominates *As I Lay Dying* much the way Caddy dominates *The Sound and the Fury*; she is the hub, the center, around whom the other characters orbit. Her monologue occurs two-thirds of the way into the novel, after her death, and tells the story of her life, explaining important elements of the family dynamics. She was a schoolteacher who "took" Anse in marriage, not out of love as much as loneliness, but she found herself even more lonely until her first child Cash was born: "my aloneness . . . had never been violated until Cash came" (172). When her second child Darl was born, Addie felt tricked and betrayed by her husband, and her revenge was to make Anse promise to bury her with her family in Jefferson (a request that uncannily produces the ordeal of the journey to Jefferson). To Addie, Anse was dead, a conventional man who could only mouth platitudes, an embodiment of the mere "shape and echo" of dead words (174).

In Addie's monologue, she contrasts dead words with the wild blood of living. Her father had told her "the reason for living was to get ready to stay dead a long time" (169). Addie later believed that she had found the reason for living in fulfilling her "duty to the alive, to the terrible blood" (174), a category from which she excludes Anse. Before the birth of Jewel, she thinks of her first two children as "of me alone, of the wild blood boiling along the earth" (175). When she commits adultery with Reverend Whitfield, she "would think of the sin as garments which we would remove in order to shape and coerce the terrible blood" (175).

Jewel was the product of Addie's affair with Whitfield, and with his birth, "the wild blood" that connected her to Cash and Darl "boiled away" (176). After the affair had ended, she made her penance by giving Anse Dewey Dell to "negative" Jewel and Vardaman "to replace the child I had robbed him of"; in Addie's calculation "*now* [Anse] has three children that are his and not mine" (176, emphasis mine). This number is curious because it excludes two, not just one, of the children. Certainly Jewel is not Anse's son; the other excluded child is possibly Darl, who then seems to belong to neither parent.

Anse

Anse Bundren's promise to bury Addie with her family in Jefferson sets the action of the novel in motion. Yet, ironically, Anse's most defining characteristic is a lazy passivity so manipulative that it amounts to an intense passive aggressiveness and so blatant that it's a source of considerable humor in the novel. Darl reports that his father "was sick once from working in the sun when he was twenty-two years old, and he tells people that if he ever sweats, he will die" (17). Anse further contends that God intended man to stay put and not move (36). Notoriously lazy, Anse is yet a master at getting other people to do for him. Despite his repeated avowals that he "would be beholden to no man," his neighbors constantly help him out. As his neighbor Vernon Tull says, "Like most folks around here, I done holp him so much already I can't quit now" (33).

Anse is ridiculous but also malignantly selfish in the way he uses and betrays his family. He takes Jewel's beloved horse and Dewey Dell's money and commits Darl to an insane asylum on the journey to get Addie buried in Jefferson, while he rewards himself with new false teeth and a new wife. When Faulkner was asked if the story has a villain, though, he identified, not Anse, but conventionality: "If there is a villain in that story it's the convention in which . . . in that case insisted that because this woman had said, I want to be buried twenty miles away, that people would go to any trouble and anguish to get her there. . . . So if there was a villain it was the convention which gave them no out except to carry her through fire and flood twenty miles in order to follow the dying wish, which by that time to her meant nothing" (Gwynn and Blotner 112). Anse is the character in the novel most representative of the conventionality that Faulkner finds so stultifying.

Jewel

Jewel stands out in the Bundren family—he is literally a head taller than the other Bundrens (an early clue that he has a different father than his siblings). He is Addie's favorite child: "ma always whipped him and petted him more," Darl says (18). A man of action and furious energy, Jewel heroically rescues Addie's corpse from the flooded river and the burning barn. When the family enters the outskirts of Jefferson, he picks a fight with a townsman who pulls a knife and Darl has to intercede. In Jewel's only monologue in the novel, he imagines himself alone with Addie on a high hill, rolling and throwing rocks at everyone below.

Jewel is obsessed with his horse, whipping and petting the animal in a furious parallel to how Addie showed favoritism to Jewel growing up. Darl tells the story of how Jewel acquired the horse in an extended flashback just before the disastrous river crossing. The flashback reveals that, for weeks, Jewel secretly worked nights clearing a neighbor's land to earn money to buy the horse—furtive activity that Cash and Darl had assumed involved "rutting" with a woman. When Jewel's secret is finally revealed, Darl notes Addie's intensely emotional response to Jewel's keeping secrets from her, in effect replacing her in his affections with a rival: his horse.

> That night I found ma sitting beside the bed where [Jewel] was sleeping, in the dark. She cried hard, maybe because she had to cry so quiet; maybe because she felt the same way about tears she did about deceit, hating herself for doing it, hating him because she had to. And then I knew that I knew. (136)

What Darl "knew," supposedly, was that Jewel was illegitimate, although it is not revealed until Addie's monologue after the river crossing. Thus, Jewel's relationship to his horse, which Darl notes carefully, is a substitute for Jewel's close bond with Addie, a substitution summarized when Darl says to himself "Jewel's mother is a horse" (95).

Cash

The eldest of the Bundren children, Cash has only five monologues in the novel, the first three of which are focused on the coffin that he has built for Addie. In these early monologues, Cash's perfectionism as a carpenter verges on a comic monomania. The stoicism he shows when he breaks his leg in the river crossing, though, sheds new light on his character, and he emerges toward the end of the novel as an admirably balanced spokesman for the family.

53023

Cash had broken the same leg previously in a fall from a church he was building, and he already walked with a limp. He suffers having the bone set by Billy Varner, a neighbor whose only experience is treating horses; "Cash fought pretty hard for a while, until he fainted" is the laconic way another neighbor, Armstid, describes the gruesome procedure. The pain Cash endures from the second fracture is compounded by the rough wagon ride as the journey continues. In a misguided but grotesque attempt to stabilize the break temporarily, the family pours concrete on it. By the time they reach Jefferson, Cash's leg has turned black and Dr. Peabody must take off "sixty-odd square inches of skin" to remove the concrete and treat the broken leg. Cash's longsuffering endurance ennobles him even as the horror of his ordeal adds to the grotesqueness of the family's situation. Both the obsessive care he lavishes on building the coffin and the agony he experiences on the journey are unstated testaments to his love for Addie.

Cash seems the least emotionally scarred of Addie's children, perhaps because, as the first child, he received more attention from his mother than the others and yet avoided the intense suffocating bond she lavished on Jewel. He is the Bundren who is most sympathetic to Darl and has an intuitive bond with him—although he participates in the plot to have Darl committed. According to Cash, there is no excuse for Darl's burning the Gillespies' barn; he values "what a man has built with his own sweat" (238). Cash regrets Darl's incarceration, though; he acknowledges that sanity is a relative judgment and that it would have been a blessing to "get shut of [Addie's corpse] in some clean way" (233), as Darl was attempting to do. Cash tries to resolve his conflict by telling Darl that he'll be better off in a quiet place "with none of the bothering and such" (238).

Cash concludes the novel with an account of Anse introducing the duck-shaped, pop-eyed second Mrs. Bundren to her step-children. In a calm, even tone, Cash looks ahead to winters spent listening to records on Mrs. Bundren's graphophone, wishing that Darl could share their enjoyment. His final monologue provides a bizarrely mild resolution to the Bundrens' grotesque mortuary journey.

Dewey Dell

The only daughter in the Bundren family, Dewey Dell finds herself too preoccupied with her unwanted pregnancy to process her mother's death. Her father's daughter, Dewey Dell is notably passive in the way she had accepted the sexual advances of her seducer Lafe. As they picked cotton together, she told herself that if her sack is full when they reach the end of the row, she would not be able to help having sex with him. Without her saying anything, he started adding his pickings into her sack: "And so it was full when we came to the end of the row and I could not help it" (27).

Dewey Dell's predicament is poignant and her four monologues convey her distress in a lyrical stream of consciousness. With no one to turn to for assistance (Lafe's only help is to provide ten dollars, which Anse takes from her), she schemes to get an abortion. Fiercely protecting her secret, she deceives her family by bringing her Sunday clothes along on the journey in a box that she says contains cakes that she will sell for their neighbor Cora Tull in town. Dewey Dell thinks she needs to look presentable in town in order to get an abortion. Both of her attempts to get help aborting her pregnancy fail. The Mottson pharmacist Moseley refuses aid on moral grounds, and the Jefferson soda jerk Skeet MacGowan takes sexual advantage of her, telling her that the act will cause her to abort. MacGowan's trick is another example of the grotesque humor in the novel.

Dewey Dell's repetitive language reinforces her desperation, and her imagery associates her with natural rhythms, as when she feels "like a wet seed wild in the hot blind earth" (64). By emphasizing her body and her fertility, in Leslie Fiedler's estimation, Faulkner risks reducing Dewey Dell to "the peasant wench as earth goddess." Fiedler notes that her very name is allegorical, "suggesting both a natural setting and woman's sex, her sex as a fact of nature" (320). Faulkner presents Dewey Dell's unexpressed anguish so vividly, though, that he creates immense sympathy for her inarticulate distress and reveals a humanity that transcends misogynistic stereotype. Furthermore, Dewey Dell's relationship to Darl complicates her character by revealing her strong-willed, active side. Darl communicates to her without words that he knows her sexual secrets and does not judge her for them, but Dewey Dell hates him for invading her privacy. She even fantasizes killing him with a knife. When the authorities come to take him to the asylum, she jumps on him "scratching and clawing at him like a wild cat" (237), according to Cash, who suspects she was the one who told Gillespie that Darl had torched his barn. By removing Darl, the only one who knows that she is pregnant, Dewey Dell buys time but the novel leaves her situation unresolved.

Vardaman

The youngest Bundren, Vardaman functions somewhat like Benjy in *The Sound and the Fury* by providing a naïve perspective on events that prompted some early readers to assume that he shares Benjy's mental incapacity. However, Vardaman is not mentally handicapped; rather he simply has no one to explain what his mother's death means, and so he comes up with his own primitive explanation that is based on coincidence. His mother's death coincides with his catching a fish and Doctor Peabody's arrival, so Vardaman equates his mother's death with the fish's being cut up and eaten, and he blames Peabody. After he lets Peabody's team of horses loose, he runs four miles in the rain to Vernon Tull's house because he thinks that Tull (who saw the fish before it was cut up) can help him reverse his mother's death. Later, not understanding that his mother no longer breathes, Vardaman drills air holes into her coffin. His frantic efforts to make sense of what has happened culminate in his famous five-word section: "My mother is a fish."

Faulkner uses Vardaman's unsophisticated way of registering and recording what he sees as a means to describe events with immediacy and vividness. On the journey, he describes the buzzards circling and the mules drowning with a simplicity that invites the reader to fill in the horror of those images. At another extreme, Faulkner sometimes allows Vardaman to convey inchoate sensations in language that is not realistic, but instead is floridly expressive of a nonverbal awareness, as in this description of Jewel's horse in the dark barn: "It is as though the dark were resolving him out of his integrity, into an unrelated scattering of components—snuffings and stampings; smells of cooling flesh and ammoniac hair; an illusion of a co-ordinated whole of splotched hide and strong bones within which, detached and secret and familiar, an *is* different from my *is*" (56).

Darl seems to be the only family member with the patience to communicate with Vardaman on his unconventional level. Their dialogues disclose a touching intimacy between the man slipping toward madness and the traumatized child. After one of these conversations over Addie's coffin, Vardaman keeps repeating that he has seen something (presumably Darl setting fire to the Gillespies' barn) that Dewey Dell says he is "not to tell nobody" (214–17). Vardaman's 10 monologues (second in frequency only to Darl's) provide valuable continuity to the novel and add to its compelling strangeness.

The Tulls and Other Narrators

The Bundrens' nearest neighbors, Vernon and Cora Tull, and various other neighbors and townspeople round out the cast of narrators in *As I Lay Dying*. Hypocrisy and unreliability are the keynotes of Cora's judgments of Addie and her children, and yet her small-minded, gossipy commentary provides comic relief. Vernon Tull speaks for the community of farmers who generously come to the aid of the Bundrens, even as they complain about Anse's fecklessness. In Vernon's six monologues (the most allocated to any person outside the Bundren family), he describes such key events as the completion of Addie's coffin and her funeral, and his presence at the disastrous river crossing allows him to be one of the narrators of the novel's most dramatic episode.

Reverend Whitfield's single monologue, which follows Cora's final one and Addie's solitary one, forms a triptych that hems in Addie's fierce integrity with hypocritical cant on both sides. Whitfield, afraid that Addie will reveal their adultery on her deathbed, vows to admit it first, but when Addie dies without having confessed, he conveniently interprets it as God's forgiveness and acceptance of "the will for the deed" of confession (179). Other narrators seem to be delivering spoken dramatic monologues to implied listeners rather than the internal monologues of the Bundrens. These include Doctor Peabody, the neighbors Armstid and Samson, and the two men to whom Dewey Dell turns for help (Moseley and MacGowan). These narrators from outside the family collectively serve to place the Bundrens in their social context, opening up their intensely solipsistic world to somewhat more objective scrutiny.

THEMES

Some of the themes of *As I Lay Dying* have been introduced in the preceding discussions of structure and character. One is the tension between collective action (the common goal of the family as well as the community to bury Addie) and selfish individual concerns (emphasized by the novel's fragmented monologue structure); another is the tension between Anse's conventionality and Addie's covert rejection of it. Two other major themes are encapsulated in the terms liminality and language.

Liminality refers to the condition of being in between two states (the word stems from the Latin word for threshold, *limen*), such as being between night and day or life and death or, in an anthropological sense, the period during a rite of passage in which a person is "betwixt and between" social roles such as adolescent and adult. The title *As I Lay Dying* itself denotes a liminal state of being between life and death, and the course of the novel traces the extended process of Addie's death and burial during which her corpse in the coffin retains an uncanny animation for her family. For example, Darl and Vardaman "can hear her inside the wood" of the coffin, and they ask what she is saying (214). Addie's monologue, which occurs after her death, places her in the liminal position of a dead woman speaking. Similarly, for much of the novel, Darl seems to occupy a liminal position between sanity and insanity, and Dewey Dell's illegitimate pregnancy suspends her between girlhood and motherhood.

The theme of liminality in the novel emphasizes the burial journey as an extended rite of passage. According to anthropological theories of ritual, the liminal stage of a rite of passage is a zone in which conventional social norms are temporarily inverted. In *As I Lay Dying*, the family's liminal status as mourners gives them permission to roam the countryside imposing on neighbors, even to the point of causing outrage over the smell of Addie's decomposing body. In rites of passage, though, as in the novel, the disorder of the liminal stage gives way to a reincorporation into conventionally structured society. Once Addie is buried and Darl is committed to the insane asylum (to redress the burning of the Gillespie barn), Anse remarries and the Bundren family returns to a semblance of normalcy. However, the experience of liminality provides participants in ritual an opportunity to learn about alternatives to normalcy, such as when Cash reflects about Darl's insanity that he "aint so sho that ere a man has the right to say what is crazy and what aint" (238). Liminality offers at least a glimpse of other ways of structuring society, and some theorists argue that it even can subvert established order (Carlson 19).

Another major theme of *As I Lay Dying* is the question of the efficacy of language. Addie claims "words are no good; that words don't ever fit even what they are trying to say at," that a word like love is "just a shape to fill a lack" (171–72). She opposes words—which "go straight up in a thin line, quick and harmless"—with "how terribly doing goes along the earth, clinging to it" (173). André Bleikasten, however, points out the irony that Addie's indictment of language is itself expressed in language: "language is here at once the target, the arrow, and the bow" (*Ink of Melancholy* 204). Addie expresses Faulkner's own ambivalence about language, but in the process overstates the case. Faulkner shares "the modern yearning for the unsayable," according to Bleikasten (206), but he never forsakes trying to "reconcile silence with speech, experience with form, life with art, his unflagging effort to build the reality of his work on the unreality of words and his never-dying hope to turn fictions into truths" (207).

Bleikasten summarizes the theme of language in the novel as the parable of the carpenter (Cash) and the madman (Darl). He sees Cash's perfectionist approach to the craft of carpentry as emblematic of the craftsmanship of a good writer who lacks artistic vision. Without such a vision what is produced is empty, a coffin-like shape to fill a lack. Darl, on the other hand, possesses a mad poet's vision—his "queer" eyes are full of the land, as we are repeatedly told, and he sees the hidden secrets of his family—but he lacks an outlet for what he sees. Bleikasten sees Darl as "Faulkner's portrait of the novelist-poet . . . except that he is a poet without poems, a novelist without novels, an artist without an *oeuvre*" (*Ink of Melancholy* 209). Language is elusive but Faulkner remains committed to using it to meld craft and vision into a quest for truth.

ALLUSIONS

One tool of Faulkner's craft is intertextuality, his acknowledgement of literary tradition through allusion to previous texts and writers. The title *As I Lay Dying* refers to Book XI of Homer's *Odyssey* as translated by Sir William Marris. The phrase occurs when Odysseus visits Hades, the underworld, and encounters the shade of Agamemnon, the fallen Greek leader who was the brother-in-law of Helen of Troy. Agamemnon tells how, as he lay dying, the victim of his murderous wife Clytemnestra, she shamelessly turned away from him "and scorned/To draw my eyelids down or close my mouth" (Luce 1). The Bundren family repeats the patterns of adultery, betrayal, and revenge set in motion in the Greek legends of the House of Atreus (Agamemnon's father), a cycle of violence that stretched across three generations. Addie speaking from the dead echoes the situation of Agamemnon in Homer's epic.

An American literary source to which Faulkner alludes in his novel is Nathaniel Hawthorne's *The Scarlet Letter.* In Hawthorne's novel, Hester Prynne, like Addie, commits adultery with a man of God and bears a child named Pearl, whose name suggests a preciousness like Jewel's in *As I Lay Dying.* Just as Hester wore the scarlet letter A for adultery as an emblem of her sin, Addie says that she thought of herself and Whitfield as dressed in garments of sin.

Dianne C. Luce traces further detailed allusions in *As I Lay Dying* in her volume of annotations to the novel. She explores cases in which characters such as Anse, Cora, and Whitfield hypocritically refer to passages from the Bible, with Anse identifying with Job and Whitfield with Christ. At other times, Addie's monologue echoes T. S. Eliot's *The Waste Land.* Compare her statement that "In the early spring it was worst" (170) with Eliot's "April is the cruellest month." Darl refers to a pornographic image of "a woman and a pig with two backs and no face" (254), a reference to the "beast with two backs" as a sexual image in act I, scene i of William Shakespeare's *Othello.* Faulkner incorporates a rich array of allusions in the novel, in both broad and specific ways.

ALTERNATIVE READING: PERFORMANCE STUDIES

Performance studies scholars Beverly Whitaker Long and Mary Frances HopKins cite definitions of *performing* that include "executing," "fulfilling," "completing," and "finishing." "In each case," they write, "the plain-speaking synonym is simply 'doing'" (ix). Performance studies is an evolving set of interdisciplinary approaches to cultural doings in wide-ranging contexts that include theatrical and literary events, everyday life interactions, and public ceremonies. Richard Schechner explains that "Performance must be construed as a 'broad spectrum' or 'continuum' of human actions ranging from ritual, play, sports, popular entertainments, the performing arts (theatre, dance, music), and everyday life performances to the enactment of social, professional, gender, race, and class roles, and on to healing (from shamanism to surgery), the media, and the internet. . . . The underlying notion is that any action that is framed, presented, highlighted, or displayed is a performance" (2). Applying a performance studies perspective to As I Lay Dying involves exploring how the text as a generative force enacts and interrogates culture, power, and ways of being (Madison and Hamera); this entails performing As I Lay Dying in several senses.

Faulkner's novel has a history of being literally enacted on the stage in adaptations that constitute embodied interpretations of the text. In 1935, the French actor Jean-Louis Barrault staged the novel under the title Autour d'une Mere ("Around a Mother") in a performance that combined mime and spoken text. Barrault himself played both Jewel and Addie, enacting Jewel on his horse as a centaur-like figure and presenting Addie as "a sort of idol or totem, impersonating her stripped to the waist over a flared skirt, wearing a mask and an enormous black wig" (Bleikasten, Faulkner's As I Lay Dying 144). Barrault performed the novel as drama stripped to its primitive ritualistic state. In 1948, the choreographer Valerie Bettis created a dance version of As I Lay Dying that remained a successful part of her repertoire for over a decade and was presented on television in 1965. With music by Bernardo Segall, Bettis shaped the dance as a narrative of Addie's memories of events in her life.

The novel has also been adapted as a play by Robert Flynn in the 1960s, Peter Gill in 1985, and Frank Galati in 1995. Flynn's adaptation at Baylor University in 1960 added few lines to Faulkner's text, relying mostly on rearrangement to translate the novel's fragmented structure into a more linear dramatic action focused on the image of the wagon bearing Addie's coffin on the burial journey. Director Paul Baker noted, "The wagon became for us as we worked on this play a great kind of stage poetry without words. The movement of the wagon, the turning of the wheels, and the family on their journey to bury the mother was for us a poetic statement of time and humanity, and of Faulkner's vision of life" (qtd. in Logan 30). The production was revised in subsequent productions at the Dallas

Theater Center and on tour in Paris in 1964. Peter Gill adapted and directed his starkly stylized production for the National Theatre in London, mostly retaining the monologue structure of the novel, according to reviewers. Frank Galati, a professor of performance studies at Northwestern University, adapted and directed his 1995 Steppenwolf Theatre Company production in Chicago with Faulkner's language uppermost in his mind. "At the center of this book," Galati noted, "and what makes it so galvanizing to think about in terms of theatrical performance is . . . hearing Faulkner's remarkable language sung on stage, spoken in time and embodied by a living interpreter" (qtd. in Antonio).

Another sense in which *As I Lay Dying* can be experienced as a performance is provided by speech act theory as developed by J. L. Austin and elaborated by John Searle. Speech act theory posits two types of utterance: constatives, which describe reality in true or false terms, and performatives, statements that attempt to do something as a result of their being uttered, such as "I promise." André Bleikasten asks, "Is the entire action of [*As I Lay Dying*] not the direct result of what today linguists would call a speech act, that is, a vow, a promise, Anse's *word* to Addie? Utterances can be acts" (*Ink of Melancholy* 204). Approaching the novel as a complex of speech acts clarifies the generative force of an utterance that produces the Bundren family's journey to Jefferson and all its consequences; furthermore, on the journey we hear Darl state "Jewel's mother is a horse" and Vardaman say "My mother is a fish." Although these utterances ostensibly describe Addie in literally false terms, they forcefully express for Jewel and Vardaman their transformation of her into a substitute for her absence.

A final possible performative reading of *As I Lay Dying* is to hear Darl as role-playing all the other voices in the novel. This is one way to explain his clairvoyance and his centrality in the novel; he conjures and ventriloquizes the voices in a tour de force performance comparable to Faulkner's own. His madness, in this reading of the novel, manifests itself in "the ability to split into several personalities," according to Daniel Ferrer; "all the different monologues . . . are his 'voices,' allowing him to reconcile contradictory modes of defence against an intolerable reality" (33). As stated earlier, Darl possesses a mad poet's vision, although he lacks an outlet for it. Perhaps his gift manifests itself in such channeling and performing of voices. When asked how Darl could narrate Addie's death when he wasn't present at it, Faulkner replied:

> Who can say how much of the good poetry of the world has come out of madness, and who can say just how much of super-perceptivity . . . a mad person might not have? It may not be so, but it's nice to think that there is

some compensation for madness. That maybe the madman does see more than the sane man. That the world is more moving to him. That he is more perceptive. He has something of clairvoyance, maybe, a capacity for telepathy. Anyway, nobody can dispute it and that was a very good way, I thought, a very effective way to tell what was happening back there at home. (Gwynn and Blotner 113)

Faulkner's response connects Darl's special powers with both madness and poetry. "A trick," he concludes, "but since the whole book was a *tour de force*, I think it was a permissible trick" (113), and another permissible trick is to read *As I Lay Dying* performatively—as both Faulkner's and Darl's tour de force one-man show (Anderson).

6

Light in August (1932)

Faulkner claimed that the genesis of *Light in August* was "the idea of [a] young girl with nothing, pregnant, determined to find her sweetheart" (Gwynn and Blotner 74). The novel begins with the girl, Lena Grove, sitting beside the road to Jefferson, having come from Alabama, and thinking *"although I have not been quite a month on the road I am already in Mississippi"* (3). Five hundred pages later, the novel ends with Lena holding her newborn baby, again on the road, saying "My, my. A body does get around. Here we aint been coming from Alabama but two months, and now it's already Tennessee" (507). Lena's understated wonder frames the novel's complex mix of stories—that seem at first glance to be unrelated—with a placid pastoral calmness.

Light in August is an ambitious novel. Having been unable to repeat the ecstasy that he found writing *The Sound and the Fury*, Faulkner discovered himself "deliberately choosing among possibilities and probabilities of behavior and weighing and measuring each choice by the scale of the Jameses and Conrads and Balzacs" ("An Introduction" 1972 227). To Michael Millgate these remarks indicate that "in writing *Light in August* Faulkner set out to lay claim, once and for all, to the status of a major novelist—to measure himself quite specifically against such towering figures as Henry James, Joseph Conrad, and Honoré de Balzac—and to do so by making *Light in August* a work of stylistic eloquence, psychological depth, and magisterial scope, a 'big' novel capable of standing alongside the greatest novels of the past" (Millgate, "A Novel: Not an Anecdote" 41). In *Light in August*, Faulkner balances the experimentalism of his earlier works with the more traditional narrative conventions of recognized masters. The result is a structure of relatively conventional blocks of narrative combined in unconventional ways—a form that he would continue to refine further in subsequent works, such as *If I Forget Thee, Jerusalem* and *Go Down, Moses*.

In *Light in August*, Faulkner also incorporated elements of conventional genres. Shortly before writing it, he had extensively revised and published his sixth novel *Sanctuary,* a sensational tale of rape and murder, leading some critics to dismiss his work as part of a "cult of cruelty" (Thompson). Michael Millgate identifies a number of similarities between the two novels, notably parallel back-stories for the criminals Popeye and Joe Christmas. Just as in *Sanctuary* he worked variations on the genre of gangster stories then popular in film and fiction, in *Light in August* Faulkner incorporated the murder-mystery form, as well as elements of the classic pastoral genre (which presents rural life in an idealized form). Yet he juxtaposed these conventional elements in a typically modernist, fragmented manner.

In *Light in August*, Faulkner weaves together the stories of three social outcasts in Yoknapatawpha County. These include two major characters that never meet: the unwed rural madonna named Lena Grove and a perverse Christ figure named Joe Christmas. Linking their stories is that of Gail Hightower, a defrocked minister who, on the same day, assists with the birth of Lena's baby and witnesses the killing and mutilation of Joe Christmas. A birth and a death, the comic journey of a white girl juxtaposed with the tragic odyssey of a man who thinks he may be part black—this novel is like a loose bag of carefully opposed elements that only partially meld.

Light in August is narrated omnisciently in language that is more direct and less flowing with streams of consciousness than that of *The Sound and the Fury* and *As I Lay Dying;* yet it shares with those novels a complex multiplicity of points of view and a convoluted chronology. Most disconcertingly, *Light in August* confronts received ideas of race and gender with shockingly racist and misogynistic scenes that continue to disturb many readers. Despite—or perhaps because of—these challenging aspects, critics judge *Light in August* an undeniably great if problematic work.

SETTING

Light in August is part of Faulkner's extensive Yoknapatawpha saga. Most of the action takes place in Jefferson, the county seat, and Mottstown, a nearby community with a railroad connection to Jefferson. However, all of the major characters of *Light in August* are outsiders of various kinds to Jefferson society—they are passing through like Lena Grove, migrant temporary workers such as Joe Christmas and Lucas Burch (under the alias Joe Brown), or social pariahs like Joanna Burden and Gail Hightower. Even hardworking Byron Bunch, although he has lived in Jefferson for seven years, is still considered an outsider. The townspeople of Jefferson constitute the communal backdrop against which the major characters stand out in relief.

Peopling the landscape of the novel are various minor characters that reappear in other Faulkner works. These include the Armstids, who assist Lena Grove much the same way that they helped the Bundren family in *As I Lay Dying,* and Mrs. Beard, the Jefferson boarding-house proprietor, whose lodgers included Byron Snopes in *Sartoris* as well as Byron Bunch in *Light in August.* The Burden family that figures in the Reconstruction background of *Light in August* also appears in *The Unvanquished,* where the two Calvin Burdens (grandfather and half-brother of Joanna) are killed by Col. Sartoris.

Light in August marks the first appearance of Gavin Stevens in a Faulkner novel; he figures prominently in such later novels as *Go Down, Moses; Intruder in the Dust; Knight's Gambit;* and the Snopes trilogy (*The Hamlet, The Town,* and *The Mansion*). Stevens, the Harvard-educated Jefferson district attorney, appears in chapter 19 of *Light in August* to hypothesize about the circumstances that led Joe Christmas to make his fatal attempt to flee as he is led to trial. The character of Stevens owes something to Faulkner's friend and mentor Phil Stone in that he is a well-educated intellectual, although limited by his Southern gentility, especially in regard to racial issues.

PLOT AND STRUCTURE

As in detective fiction, Faulkner builds a main plot around a presumed murder—that of the spinster Joanna Burden—but the suspense revolves around not the identity of the murderer but his motive, and it is sustained through selective withholding of information. The omniscient narrator circles around the scene of the crime in a narrative relay that introduces us to the major characters: Lena Grove, Byron Bunch, Joe Christmas, and Gail Hightower. Hugh Ruppersburg provides a helpful chronology of the novel's events, which Faulkner presents in a complexly arranged series of flashbacks and overlapping versions from different points of view. In order to map the structural complexity of *Light in August,* it will help to trace sequentially how Faulkner juxtaposes and interweaves the three seemingly separate stories. The first chapter introduces us to Lena Grove in the late stages of pregnancy. It is August 1932, and she has traveled to Jefferson from Alabama to find and marry her soon-to-be-born child's father, Lucas Burch. As she approaches the town, in the distance is "a tall yellow column" of smoke from the burning house where (we will soon learn) Joanna Burden lies dead (30). The present action of the novel takes place over a little more than a week, starting the day before Lena's arrival.

In chapter 2, Faulkner shifts the focus to Byron Bunch, a hardworking lumber mill employee who recalls the arrivals of three strangers to the mill at intervals over a period of several years. Three years earlier, the brooding, mysterious Joe Christmas arrived to work in the mill and then, only six months before the present time of the novel, a "weakly handsome," talkative man calling himself Joe Brown also started work. In time, Byron hears that Christmas and Brown live together in a cabin behind the Burden mansion, where they distill and sell bootleg whiskey. Sometime before the events of August 1932, they both quit working at the mill. On the August day that Lena Grove, the third stranger, arrives in Jefferson (Saturday), she comes to the mill looking for Lucas Burch and finds Byron Bunch instead.

In chapter 3, Faulkner cuts to Gail Hightower's house in Jefferson. Hightower is a disgraced minister, fired from his church 25 years earlier, whom Byron Bunch has befriended. Bunch confides to Hightower that he inadvertently revealed to Lena Grove that Lucas Burch is in town using the assumed name of Joe Brown. Byron has fallen in love with Lena at first sight, and he finds himself helping her search for the man who is his rival for her affections.

In chapter 4, Faulkner continues to focus on Hightower and Bunch as Byron recounts the excitement in town resulting from the fire and the discovery of Joanna Burden's body in the burning house. Much of the chapter is Byron's oral narrative to Hightower of what Burch/Brown has revealed to the sheriff. Burch hopes to collect a $1,000 reward offered for the capture of the killer, whom he identifies as Joe Christmas, a man assumed to be white who has told Burch he believes himself to be "part nigger" (98).

Chapter 5 shifts the focus to Joe Christmas and jumps back in time to the day before the killing, presenting Joe's erratic movements on that day. The next seven chapters fill in Joe's background, providing a context for his violent actions. He was raised from an early age in a Memphis orphanage, where a mysterious janitor named Hines watched him intently for years and said that Joe was part black. When the five-year-old Joe inadvertently witnessed a dietitian having illicit sex, she tried to get him sent away to a black orphanage. Instead, Joe was adopted as a white child by a strict, harshly religious man named Simon McEachern and his wife. When McEachern discovered that the teenaged Joe was sneaking out to meet a woman, he started a fight in which Joe knocked him down and may have killed him. For the next 15 years, Joe wandered aimlessly until, at age 33, he arrived in Jefferson and began a tortured sexual relationship with Joanna Burden, a spinster of 40 who, as the descendant of Yankee abolitionists, lived isolated from the white community. The culmination of this long flashback section of the novel is the deadly confrontation between Joe Christmas and Joanna Burden shortly after midnight early Saturday morning.

The remaining nine chapters of *Light in August* alternate between the manhunt for Joe Christmas and the actions of Byron Bunch and Gail Hightower on behalf of both Lena and Joe, climaxing in the birth of Lena's baby and Joe's death. Faulkner's plot strands converge in chapter 16, when Byron brings Joe's grandparents, Mr. and Mrs. Hines, to Hightower's house to solicit help; we learn that Joe's parents were the Hineses' daughter Milly and a circus man, whom Mr. Hines murdered because he believed him to be part black. Milly died in childbirth, and her father took her baby on Christmas Eve to the orphanage in Memphis where he was given the name "Joe Christmas." This chapter leads into the birth of Lena's baby in chapter 17. The birth takes place at the cabin previously occupied by Christmas and the so-called Brown, where Lena has gone to await the arrival of the father of her baby. Hightower is summoned to assist at the birth, which evokes memories for Mrs. Hines of the birth of her grandson Joe.

What Irving Howe calls the triadic structure of *Light in August* (203) is unified through characters that connect and mirror the diffuse narrative strands of the novel. François Pitavy stresses the role of Byron Bunch, "who occupies a central position in the novel as the only person in touch with all the others, and so is capable of bringing them together" (*Faulkner's Light in August* 36). Even though Lena Grove and Joe Christmas never meet and though they deal with the world in opposing modes of trust and violence, their lives parallel each other's. As Pitavy notes, both are orphans who escape their families and "roam far and wide, the one in search of himself, the other in search of her seducer" (42). Similarly, Gail Hightower and Joanna Burden are both characters that live secluded, ostracized lives constrained by deadening religious piety. Both are also androgynous figures that defy conventional gender roles. As with Lena and Joe, these similarities heighten the dramatic tension of their contrasting fates.

Another technique that Faulkner employs to bind the loose structure of the plot is the repetition of scenes and motifs across and within the three main stories. Both Joanna Burden and Gail Hightower occupy dark houses (Faulkner used "Dark House" as the working title of the book). Windows figure prominently in all three plots—as an egress both Lena and Joe use for sexual rendezvous and a place where Hightower sits and muses. Both

McEachern and Joanna try to force Joe on his knees to pray, with violent results.

Despite various unifying techniques, Faulkner ultimately embraces fragmentation and incoherence as key to his view of both the world and his art. Each story separates again in the last three chapters of the novel, which present discreet endings to the stories of Christmas, Hightower, and Grove, respectively. "Lena may have been the germ of the novel and remain its alpha and omega," claims François Pitavy, "and Christmas may be the most absorbing character (the six chapters devoted to his life are among Faulkner's best), but Hightower in spite of his flaws and shortcomings, is the moral center" (54).

CHARACTERS

Joe Christmas and Joanna Burden

Joe Christmas and Joanna Burden form a couple whose intertwined tragic fates warrant discussing them in tandem. Faulkner deliberately shrouds the character of Joe Christmas in ambiguity and uncertainty, never making Joe's racial background clear. Throughout *Light in August,* other characters allege that Joe Christmas has black blood, although his father claimed to be Mexican and not black. Late in the novel, Doc Hines relates an incident from Joe's childhood at the orphanage in Memphis that sums up Joe's quandary about his identity. When a child of no more than five years, Joe asked a black yard man, "How come you are a nigger?" and the man retorted "'Who told you I am a nigger, you little white trash bastard?' and he says 'I aint a nigger' and the nigger says 'You are worse than that. You don't know what you are. And more than that, you won't never know. . . . [D]on't nobody but God know what you is'" (383–84).

When asked at the University of Virginia if Joe is "part Negro," Faulkner responded,

> I think that was his tragedy—he didn't know what he was, and so he was nothing. He deliberately evicted himself from the human race because he didn't know which he was. That was his tragedy, that to me was the tragic, central idea of the story—that he didn't know what he was, and there was no way possible in life for him to find out. Which to me is the most tragic condition a man could find himself in—not to know what he is and to know that he will never know. (Gwynn and Blotner 72)

Over the course of his life, Joe repeatedly experienced not belonging in either white or black communities. Raised as a white orphan, he was called a nigger by other children, according to Doc Hines. Yet Joe was not at home in the black community either. At one point during his 15 years on the road,

> He lived with Negroes, shunning white people. He ate with them, slept with them, belligerent, unpredictable, uncommunicative. He now lived as man and wife with a woman who resembled an ebony carving. At night he would lie in bed beside her, sleepless, beginning to breathe deep and hard. He would do it deliberately, feeling, even watching, his white chest arch deeper and deeper within his ribcage, trying to breathe into himself the dark odor, the dark and inscrutable thinking and being of negroes, with each suspiration trying to expel from himself the white blood and the white thinking and being. And all the while his nostrils at the odor which he was trying to make his own would whiten and tauten, his whole being writhe and strain with physical outrage and spiritual denial. (226)

According to John N. Duvall, Joe formed alternative communities of two with other outcasts, but these arrangements ultimately failed. As a teenager, when he fell in love with Bobbie Allen, a white prostitute whom he loved in spite of her profession, he confessed to her "I think I got some nigger blood in me" (196). At the time, she said that she didn't believe him. Later, she rejected him after his fight with his foster father, screaming to her employers "He told me himself he was a nigger!" (218). Duvall explains that her revealing their "community" secret is a betrayal that shatters their bond of mutual acceptance (Duvall, *Faulkner's Marginal Couple* 29). Unable to find peace with himself or others, his wanderings lead him at the age of 33 to Joanna Burden's house in Jefferson and another alternative community.

Joanna Burden was the granddaughter and half-sister of the Northern abolitionists killed by Col. Sartoris because of their work for voting rights for blacks during Reconstruction (as Faulkner would later tell again in *The Unvanquished*). As a result, she has lived all her life in Jefferson as a pariah in the old Burden home place. In keeping with her family's liberal traditions, she helped poor black people, who comprised her only society. Joanna's belief that Joe was part black was a key basis for their relationship.

When Joe Christmas arrived on the scene, he climbed into her kitchen through a window and stole food. Discovering him there, Miss Burden was utterly unalarmed. "'If it is just food you want, you will find that,' she said in a voice calm, a little deep, quite cold" (231). Later, either that night or the next, he entered the house again and sexually assaulted her, who, at the age of 40, was still a virgin. When she did not react to him at all the next day, he returned to "show her" that he was not to be ignored and assaulted her again, although she did not resist and even seemed to help him "with small changes of position of limbs when the ultimate need for help arose" (236). For months thereafter, she set out food for him in the kitchen at night, but they did not speak to one another. Joe started work at the lumber mill, living in a cabin behind Joanna's house.

Finally, she broke the impasse by coming to his cabin one night in September and telling him at length about her family. Her fanatical, violent grandfather Calvin Burden had migrated west from New England and married a French Catholic woman. Their son Nathaniel, a "small, dark vivid child who had inherited his mother's build and coloring" (242) seemed of a different race than his father; at 14 he ran away and did not return for 16 years at which time he found his father in Kansas, practicing an ardent abolitionism. The prodigal son arrived with a Mexican fiancée named Juana, "who looked enough like [Nathaniel's mother, now dead,] to have been her sister" (246). Also with them was their child Calvin, whom his grandfather called "another damn black Burden" (247). Years later, after the two Calvins (grandfather and grandson) have been killed by Col. Sartoris and Juana has died, Nathaniel sent for and married a New Hampshire woman, and when she gave birth two years later he named their child Joanna for her grandmother Juana.

In a revealing flashback, Joanna remembered Nathaniel's taking her when she was four years old to the family graveyard, unmarked to prevent the desecration of the graves by the community. Her father told Joanna that she couldn't escape the curse of racial difference. "The curse of the black race," he said, "is God's curse. But the curse of the white race is the black man who will be forever God's chosen own because He once cursed him." Joanna imagined this curse as a shadow over all white children falling "not only upon them but beneath them too . . . as if they were nailed to the cross" (253). Like her forebears, she dedicated herself to the struggle to raise the shadow with her, in her case by supporting higher education for black people. "But you can never lift [the shadow] to your level," her father admonished her, revealing his racist sense of superiority despite the family's good intentions. Like her grandfather and father, Joanna felt superior to black people and yet was intensely, even perversely, attracted to Joe, perhaps for that very reason.

Joanna's account of her family background marks the start of a new, fiercely erotic phase in her relationship with Joe, which the narrator, reflecting Joe's perception, compares to a sewer running by night (256). To Joe, it seems as if Joanna is compensating for her years of celibate repression with "wild throes of nymphomania" (259). Over the following year, the intensity of their sexual life diminishes and gives way to a third phase in which Joanna begins to talk about having a child; then, in late December, she tells him she is pregnant—although it eventually becomes clear that she is actually menopausal.

The relationship between Joe and Joanna reaches a climax when she insists that he get involved in her social work and pray with her. The tension between them escalates until each realizes that only death can resolve it. Joanna tries to shoot Joe (apparently planning to kill herself also), but her ancient pistol fails to fire. At this point in chapter 12, Faulkner cuts away. It is elsewhere in the novel that the reader learns that Joe responded by cutting Joanna's throat with a razor so violently that he almost severed her head.

Faulkner leaves the nature of this key episode ambiguous. John Duvall argues that technically Joe killed Joanna in self-defense, highlighting that the community's labeling him a "nigger murderer" is "doubly twisted" in that he may be neither part black nor a murderer (24). Furthermore, Joanna's willing complicity in their sexual relationship and her violent action against Joe challenge the dominant cultural image of white womanhood as passive victim of a rapacious black beast. The Jefferson community, though, "interprets Joanna and Joe in a way that . . . affirms the community's grossest stereotypes concerning the black man and Southern womanhood" (Duvall, *Faulkner's Marginal Couple* 35).

As Faulkner put it, Joe "evicted himself from the human race" because he did not know who he was. He could never find the peace that he sought (115). Part of his tragedy was that he loved Joanna Burden and rejected the potential peace and security that their unconventional life together offered. John Duvall explains:

> Joanna, of course, wants to write Joe into the continuing Burden family saga of the white man's burden, but Joe will have none of it. When she first broaches the subject of having a child, Joe would seem to have a means to achieve his goal of peace, and an inner voice flashes on him: "*Why not? It would mean ease, security, for the rest of your life. You would never have to move again,*" but the stronger self-reliant voice answers: "*No. If I give in now, I will deny all the thirty years that I have lived to make me what I chose to be*" [265]. What Christmas does not realize is that his choice to live as he does is really no choice at all, but the overdetermined product resulting from a series of incidents beyond his control. (Duvall, *Faulkner's Marginal Couple* 32)

According to Duvall, Joe succumbs to patriarchal lessons condemning female sexuality and romantic love that he learned growing up. His choices are determined by "internalized male voices that interpret his earlier frustrated desire to marry Bobbie" (33), such as that of his puritanical foster father Simon McEachern. Joe has internalized the racist and misogynistic attitudes arrayed around him, thus determining his destructive actions and his death.

After killing Joanna, Joe roams aimlessly for several days through the countryside, discovering a sense of peace in nature. "'That was all I wanted,' he thinks, in a quiet and slow amazement. 'That was all, for thirty years'" (331). He wanders "as though he desires to see his native earth in all its phases for the first or last time," achieving "peace and unhaste and quiet" (338). In this state, he catches a ride into Mottstown and allows himself to be apprehended.

In Mottstown, Doc and Mrs. Hines hear of their grandson's capture and impending trial in Jefferson. A crazed religious fanatic, Doc Hines tries to incite a mob to lynch Joe, and his meek wife doggedly attempts to protect the grandson she has not seen since shortly after his birth. In Jefferson, Mrs. Hines manages to see Joe in his jail cell, although we do not learn what transpires between them. Perhaps she tells him to seek refuge with Rev. Hightower, because, when he is led in handcuffs across the town square—supposedly to plead guilty and avoid execution—he bolts and runs to Hightower's house. Pursued by an extremist deputy named Percy Grimm, Joe finds a gun and barricades himself behind a table in Hightower's kitchen. Grimm shoots him five times and then castrates him with a butcher knife. "For a long moment he looked up at them with peaceful and unfathomable and unbearable eyes" and then "the pent black blood seemed to rush . . . out of his pale body like the rush of sparks from a rising rocket; upon that black blast the man seemed to rise soaring into their memories forever and ever" (464–65).

Joe Christmas and Joanna Burden thus both meet violent ends, their encounter a fatal collision of two lives under the same shadow of racism, according to André Bleikasten. From childhood they are "marked out for suffering and disaster. Joanna will never escape from the 'black shadow,' nor will Joe ever cease to perceive himself through the hate-filled eyes of a white" (Bleikasten, "The Closed Society and Its Subjects" 87).

Lena Grove, Byron Bunch, and Lucas Burch/Joe Brown

Lena Grove's story in outline is similar to that of Dewey Dell Bundren in *As I Lay Dying*. She is a simple country girl, motherless and unmarried, who finds herself pregnant and goes on a journey to try to solve her problem. Quietly deflecting the moral judgments that the people of Jefferson make about her unwed pregnancy, Lena exhibits an innocent trust that attracts help from strangers. Displaying a more appealing version of Anse Bundren's passive aggressiveness, her passive willfulness also takes her to Jefferson to fulfill a man's promise (to marry her as opposed to Anse's promise to bury his wife) and brings her as well to a substitute spouse (the novel ends with the presumption that she will marry Byron Bunch).

Lena is attuned to natural rhythms; "she has traveled for four weeks with the untroubled unhaste of a change of season" (52). Her pregnancy links her to the fecundity of nature, and Faulkner endows her with the mythic quality of a pagan goddess. In his talks at the University of Virginia, he compared her lack of shame about her unwed pregnancy to that of the women "on whom Jupiter begot children" (Gwynn and Blotner 199), a reminder that her name is a variation of the mythic Helen, who was the daughter of Leda from Jupiter in the form of a swan. Judith Bryant Wittenberg writes, "Lena seems at one and the same time an uncomprehending peasant with strong survival instincts and an elusive, almost mythic presence" (Wittenberg "Woman" 116).

Lena's serenity and the romantic comedy of her story are a crucial counterweight to the violence and tragedy of the story of Joe Christmas. Although she is also a morally suspect outsider in Jefferson, the community's response to her contrasts starkly with their response to Joe, bringing into vivid relief his alienation. She elicits an especially intense reaction from the three other outsiders to Jefferson who connect her to Joe Christmas: Byron Bunch, Lucas Burch/Joe Brown, and Gail Hightower.

Byron Bunch is a nondescript man over thirty so unprepossessing that one observer sums him up as "the kind of fellow you wouldn't see the first glance if he was alone by himself in the bottom of a empty concrete swimming pool" (495). A man of regular habits, Bunch works hard at the lumber mill and serves as a rural church choirmaster. Although he has lived and worked in Jefferson for seven years, he resides in Mrs. Beard's boarding house and his only friend seems to be the disgraced and reclusive former minister, Gail Hightower. What most distinguishes Bunch in the conservative community of Jefferson is his openness to unconventional people—not only Hightower but also the Hineses and Lena Grove. He falls in love with Lena at first sight, "contrary to all the tradition of his austere and jealous country raising which demands in the object physical inviolability" (49). Only briefly, when he first sees her with her newborn baby, does he feel conflicted about her sexual history. Faulkner largely renders his courtship of Lena in a vein of low romantic comedy that contrasts with Joe Christmas's tortured affairs with Bobbie Allen and Joanna Burden.

Byron's rival for Lena, Lucas Burch/Joe Brown, although handsome, is a transparently callow opportunist whose schemes are viewed with sarcastic scorn by the town. However, by labeling Joe Christmas as a nigger, he successfully diverts attention from his own illicit activity and sets in motion the manhunt that leads to Joe's death. When, at Byron's instigation, Burch is tricked into confronting Lena and their baby, he reacts with his typical bluster and bolts. At the novel's end, Byron and Lena are still ostensibly in pursuit of him, but from a traveling furniture dealer's ribald account of giving them a ride, Lena presumably has accepted Byron's courtship of her.

Gail Hightower

The third major strand of *Light in August* centers around Gail Hightower, a man who has isolated himself in his dilapidated house as if in a tower. He sits in a window and observes the world of Jefferson, and he thinks of himself as outside of life until Byron Bunch brings him into contact with the life-and-death struggles of Lena Grove and Joe Christmas.

Twenty-five years earlier, Hightower came to Jefferson as a new minister, having recently emerged from seminary with a degree and a bride. He had sought an appointment in Jefferson because his grandfather had died there in a Civil War raid on a henhouse—an undignified death that Hightower obsessively insists on viewing as glorious. This obsession causes his congregation to think him strange, and it results in his neglecting his wife until she commits suicide in a scandalous way. Fired by the church, Hightower stays on in Jefferson and becomes a target of the Ku Klux Klan because of rumors of a liaison with his black male cook. After he endures a beating by the Klan, the town ignores Hightower and he feels that he has "bought immunity" from life with his suffering (311).

Byron Bunch visits him several times a week. Having met Lena, Byron confides his love for her to Hightower, but Hightower advises him to avoid getting involved. After he meets the Hineses, Byron brings them to Hightower and asks him to save their grandson Joe Christmas with a false alibi, which Hightower refuses to do. Yet, against his better judgment, Hightower ends up acting as a midwife at the birth of Lena's baby, and he later claims that Joe "was with me the night of the murder" (464) in a vain effort to prevent the killing of Christmas.

In the novel's penultimate chapter, Hightower reflects back on his life in a long reverie. Like Joanna Burden, he was the product of an eccentric, obsessive family, leaving him isolated and shunned in adulthood. "In the end," Alwyn Berland explains, "he comes to realize that his great sin has been the rejection of his wife, who had offered him love" (50). Instead he lived vicariously: "if I am my dead grandfather on the instant of his death, then . . . [I am] the debaucher and murderer of my grandson's wife" (491). This torturously painful realization releases him into a vision of the faces of his wife, his congregation, of Byron and Lena, and Joe Christmas: "They are peaceful, as though they have escaped into an apotheosis; his own is among them" (491). But Joe's face blurs with that of his killer Percy Grimm, and Hightower feels himself emptying, floating, possibly dying. As night falls, he hears "the wild bugles and the clashing sabers and the dying thunder of hooves" (493). They are the glorious ghostly sounds of his grandfather's dying charge.

The resolution of Hightower's story in *Light in August* is highly ambiguous. Some critics, such as Cleanth Brooks, assume that his involvement with Lena Grove and Joe Christmas restores him to the community from which he had been long estranged. "These are, however, very minimal actions," according to Alexander Welsh. "[Hightower's] belated effort to save Christmas is as useless as it is feeble, and considering everything we are made to understand about Grove, it is hard to believe that she would not have given birth to a healthy child without assistance" (Welsh 134). For Welsh, Hightower never becomes more than a grotesque outsider to the community: "old and flabby and cuckolded, he is so marginal as to be tolerated by his neighbors in Jefferson only in the way in which, anthropologists tell us, communities tolerate certain persons as shameless ones" (131). His story functions ultimately in the novel as a nonviolent but still death-obsessed complement to Joe Christmas's alienation. Both men rejected love and were evicted from society—Christmas violently and Hightower more passively. Only Hightower, though, ultimately takes moral responsibility for his actions, justifying Pitavy's claim that in spite of his weaknesses he remains the novel's moral center.

THEMES

Major interlocking themes in *Light in August* involve the effect of religion, sexuality, and race on the lives of the characters and the roles that these dimensions of the human condition play in shaping—and warping—identity. The story of Joe Christmas carries much of the weight of these themes, but they are developed in the other strands of the novel as well.

In *Light in August*, religion often manifests itself as a puritanical concern with the inherent depravity of man (and especially of woman) and the stern punishment for sin. Alwyn Berland identifies "the religious and cultural residue of Puritan doctrine" that Faulkner attacks in the novel as "not simply the theology of a particular region, but rather a set of attitudes, beliefs, and cultural practices that have been inherited from earlier religious doctrine" (33–34). Faulkner represents several patriarchal figures in *Light in August* as judgmental religious zealots obsessed with original sin. These include Joe Christmas's grandfather Doc Hines, his foster father Simon McEachern, and Joanna Burden's grandfather. Even Lena Grove's brother responds to her pregnancy by calling her a whore (6). Hines and McEachern are especially rabid in their fanaticism, instilling in Joe Christmas a strain of Puritanism in spite of his rebelliousness toward McEachern. As a small child, Joe learns to expect harsh punishment for misdeeds and to associate femininity with filth and illness.

One of Joe's earliest memories involves a kind of primal scene of a dietitian at the orphanage having sex with a medical interne. Five years old, Joe had often stolen into the dietitian's room to sneak a taste of toothpaste. Hearing her approaching on the day in question, he hid behind a curtain while she had a tryst with the interne. Having swallowed too much of the dietitian's toothpaste, he became sick to his stomach and vomited. When the dietitian dragged him from his hiding place, he expected to be punished. Instead, a few days later, she tried to bribe him not to tell on her. Not understanding, he didn't respond, and she then denounced him to the matron in charge of the orphanage as a "nigger," leading to his being sent away with the McEacherns.

At the time, Joe did not understand what the dietitian and interne had been doing—the chapter famously begins with the sentence "Memory believes before knowing remembers" (119)—but the experience linked the dietitian's "soft womansmelling garments" (121) behind the curtain with being sick to his stomach. Later, in adolescence, when he learned from an older boy about menstruation, the information disturbed him to the point that he killed a sheep and washed his hands in its blood in an instinctive ritual of purification (185). Most tellingly, when his girlfriend Bobbie Allen later told him one night she could not have sex with him because she was menstruating, he ran away into some woods.

> He reached the woods and entered, among the hard trunks, the branch-shadowed quiet, hardfeeling, hardsmelling, invisible. In the notseeing and the hardknowing as though in a cave he seemed to see a diminishing row of suavely shaped urns in moonlight, blanched. And not one was perfect. Each one was cracked and from each crack there issued something liquid, deathcolored, and foul. He touched a tree, leaning his propped arms against it, seeing the ranked and moonlit urns. He vomited. (189)

Joe internalized a puritanical attitude toward female sexuality to such a degree that he associated sex and women with filth. "In *Light in August*,"

François Pitavy notes, "the images and symbols used to associate feminin-ity and evil abound in great wealth—images of decay, of sewers and fear-some abysses, of thick, black, filthy water, and of death. For in Joe's eyes women are equivalent to corruption" (*Faulkner's* Light in August 101).

Race is also implicated in Joe's disgust for women's sexuality. "For Joe, as for his grandfather," as Pitavy explains, "Man and White are of God, while Woman and Black are of the Devil. The Negro world and the female world are both moist and dark, overpowering, clinging, smother-ing" (*Faulkner's* Light in August 98). In chapter 5, before killing Joanna Burden, Joe walks through Freedman Town, a black neighborhood. "It was as though he and all other manshaped life about him had been re-turned to the lightless hot wet primogenitive Female," and he escapes into "the cold hard air of white people" (115). Joe yearns for clearly de-fined limits to prevent his feeling engulfed by femininity and blackness, but the ambiguity of his racial background leaves him stranded in an undefined twilight zone.

Eric J. Sundquist identifies Joe's uncertain race in the novel as a sym-bol of the fear of miscegenation, the amalgamation of white and black races. This fear manifests itself in a racist cultural fantasy of so-called black beasts lusting after white women. Motivating this fantasy, according to Sundquist, is a guilt-ridden denial of the obverse fact that in slavery, white masters often raped their black slave women, thereby fathering children of mixed race. He describes "the climate of fantasy the book assumes and depends on for its power" as "a willful blindness to what clearly exists (the historical fact of the rape of black women by white men during and af-ter slavery) and a hallucinatory frenzy about what exists more in fantasy than in fact (the inexorable craving for and rape of white women by black men)" (Sundquist 76).

The idea of miscegenation connects the divergent plot lines of *Light in August* in what Sundquist calls "the single link between Christmas and Lena Grove" and "the most improbable, haunting, and necessary scene in the book[:] When [Mrs. Hines] mistakes Lena's baby for her grandson . . . and Lena's consequent confusing of Christmas himself with the child's fa-ther" (75). Lena confesses the latter confusion to Hightower: "[Mrs. Hines] keeps on talking about him like his pa was that . . . the one in jail, that Mr Christmas. She keeps on, and then I get mixed up and it's like sometimes I cant—like I am mixed up too and I think that his pa is that Mr—Mr Christmas too—" (409). This sense of racial confusion is compounded by Byron Bunch's description of the actual father, Lucas Burch/Joe Brown, as "dark complected" (55) and the Burden family having dark coloring from their Gallic and Mexican bloodlines.

In these ways, Faulkner subtly evokes the dominant culture's nightmare of racial amalgamation that Sundquist identifies as the source of the novel's power to haunt its readers. The same vague fear hovers in the rumors that Joe's father is part black—Mrs. Hines attributes the rumor to the owner of the circus that employed him, saying "it was just that circus man that said he was a nigger and maybe he never knew for certain" (378)—and over Joanna Burden's hoped-for pregnancy with Joe's child. "A full measure," she muses. "Even to a negro bastard child. I would like to see father's and Calvin's faces" (266).

Themes of Puritanism, sexism, and racism blend and interlock in *Light in August*. Each thematic strain depends upon a dualism of opposed elements (the elect and the damned, masculine and feminine, white and black) in which the first term in each pair is valued over the second, abased term. According to André Bleikasten, what makes Joe Christmas most threatening to the community of Jefferson is that he undermines the very idea of such clear-cut divisions.

> What makes "the folks so mad" [350] is not the presumed miscegenation, the guilty mixture of black and white blood, but the lack in Christmas of any trace of miscegenation, the visible invisibility of his blackness. This "nigger" is white; the blackness in his whiteness cannot be ascertained. Neither his physical aspect nor his style of behavior conforms to racist stereotypes. Now if a black man can look and act exactly like a white man, if appearances fail to match and confirm essences, whiteness and blackness alike become shady notions, and once the white/black opposition has broken down, the whole social structure threatens to crumble. Christmas is thus a living challenge to the community's elemental norms and categories. Whether on purpose or not, whether knowingly or not, he subverts its either/or logic, draws attention to the fragility of the law, and points to the unacknowledged origin of racism by showing it up as a *cosa mentale*, a mere thing of the mind. (*"Light in August:* The Closed Society and Its Subjects" 97–98)

Just as Joe Christmas destabilizes racial distinctions, Joanna Burden's androgyny and Gail Hightower's suspect relationships with men destabilize normative gender roles. The themes of race and gender in *Light in August* combine with the novel's critique of Puritanism to challenge the dualism characteristic of Western thinking.

SYMBOLS AND ALLUSIONS

In addition to the symbols and images that associate femininity and filth (such as the cracked urn) and those evoking miscegenation previously discussed, a major symbol in *Light in August* is inherent in the title. Light and dark images recur throughout the book, highlighted most prominently in the symbolism of shadows. Joanna Burden reveals to Joe Christmas that, as a child, she came to see black people as "a shadow in which I lived, we lived, all white people, all other people. . . . And I seemed to see the black shadow in the shape of a cross" (253). Joe Christmas embodies this shadow, becoming her white (wo)man's burden, the cross upon which she is crucified. Climbing out of his bedroom window to meet Bobbie, he moved "with the shadowlike agility of a cat" and passed "swift as a shadow across the window where the [McEacherns] slept" (170). Running away from her when she tells him she is menstruating, Joe "faded on down the road, the shape, the shadow" (189). Climbing into Joanna Burden's kitchen window for the first time, "he seemed to flow into the dark kitchen: a shadow returning without a sound and without loco-motion to the allmother of obscurity and darkness" (230). Finally, after Percy Grimm has shot and castrated him, "He just lay there, with his eyes open and empty of everything save consciousness, and with something, a shadow, about his mouth" (464).

Character names signal another source of symbolism and allusion in the novel. Lena Grove's first name, as mentioned earlier, evokes the pagan Helen of Troy, an archetype of the eternal feminine, and her last name suggests her connection to nature. It is hard to overlook parallels between Joe Christmas and his namesake Jesus Christ. Joe is deposited at the or-phanage on Christmas Eve; in his last week, his disciple-like roommate Joe Brown betrays him for money; he suffers without complaint being struck in the face when discovered in Mottstown; in death, his blood spurts up "like the rush of sparks from a rising rocket" and his image ascends "soaring into [the witnesses'] memories forever and ever" (465). Yet, François Pitavy rightly insists "Christmas is an ironic version of Christ, as his life is one of hatred and violence towards men" (*Faulkner's* Light in August 77).

ALTERNATE READING: IDEOLOGICAL CRITICISM

Ideological criticism grew out of Marxist theory, which holds that mate-rial conditions shape individual subjectivity—"that those with wealth in society also control the means for making wealth" and that the resulting division of society into economic classes "shapes who we are and what we can do in life" (Rivkin and Ryan 231–32). Extending Karl Marx's ideas, Antonio Gramsci argued that dominant cultural networks, and not just material conditions, oppress groups of people by winning their unwitting consent. Hegemony is Gramsci's term for the power exerted by dominant classes over oppressed groups through the latter's uncoerced acceptance of the dominant group's ideals (Gramsci 277).

Ideological critics examine the ways that hegemonic forces influence individuals through the interactive relationship between their subjective minds and objective social conditions. Theorist Louis Althusser posited that ideology "represents the imaginary relationship of individuals to their real conditions of existence" (294). Althusser further theorized that ideological state apparatuses, such as educational and religious institutions, win uncoerced acceptance of dominant ideas through a process of interpellation or hailing. This process is analogous to the way in which, when someone says "Hey, you there!" one responds automatically as the "you" named. Interpellation affects an individual's sense of identity. In this way, dominant classes call on oppressed groups to accept without question that the way things are is the way they are supposed to be.

Kevin Railey explains the ideological process of identity formation in straightforward terms:

> Althusser stresses that to become a subject—someone about whom others can speak—individuals need to be given a name, an identity of some sort. Individuals can only become recognized by others when their actions and words become identifiable by some meaningful structure, when they enact some ideology. . . . In simple terms, this process says that if I refuse to perform those activities that define me as a professor, a doctor, an accountant, a father, then people will have difficulty identifying me as such, and I too will have difficulty identifying myself. . . . One can indeed refuse to become identified by the socio-historical ideologies of one's time; however, then one will have extreme difficulty attaining any identity at all. One will essentially be invisible, as a subject, to others. (Railey 30)

Railey's explanation aptly describes the identity formation of Joe Christmas in *Light in August*. Until he accepts the identity by which society interpellates him, he is invisible. Accepting it, though, is a deadly proposition for him.

In the novel, for example, society, which initially interpellates Joe Christmas as white, affords him a privileged identity according to the dominant ideology of that time. He grows up in a white orphanage and is adopted by the white McEacherns. At the age of five, in the scene discussed earlier, Joe asks the yard man at the orphanage, "How come you are a nigger?" (383). Joe is vaguely aware of the stigma associated with being a "nigger" but does not fully understand it. The janitor perceives Joe as white ("you little white trash bastard") as does Joe himself ("I aint a nigger"). However, other children at the orphanage call Joe "nigger," and the dietitian, in her rage at his catching her in a compromising position, refers to him as a "nigger bastard" (125). Joe is caught in the middle.

When Joe falls in love with Bobbie, he tells her "I got some nigger blood in me," but stops short of identifying himself as a "nigger." Her response, "You're what?" (not "You *have* what?"), momentarily identifies him as black, before she says she doesn't believe it. Joe then qualifies his previous statement, saying "I dont know. I believe I have" (196–97), thereby distancing himself from the interpellation and implicitly refusing it. However, when Bobbie later renounces him, her claim to have "always treated you like you were a white man" (217) reveals that she had indeed thought of him as black. After this, Joe tries living alternately as a white and a black man, tricking "white men into calling him a negro in order to fight them" and conversely fighting "the negro who called him white" (225). He has been interpellated as white in a binary ideology of race, though, to the extent that when he tries "to breathe into himself . . . the dark and inscrutable thinking and being of negroes" and "to expel from himself the white blood and the white thinking and being," "his whole being [would] writhe and strain with physical outrage and spiritual denial" (225–26). Within a binary racial ideology that allows no middle ground, his parchment-colored skin marks him as white, and he is interpellated as white from an early age, even though he has doubts about it. The ideological environment provides no option of a mixed-race category that is not white or black, much less an option in which race simply does not matter. In this state of tension, Joe meets Joanna Burden, a white woman who, unlike Bobbie, treats him like a black man, even though he admits he doesn't know if he has black blood or not.

As Althusser theorized, an imaginary relationship exists between Joe and the real conditions of his existence, an ideology of race that interpellates him as first white and then black. At various points, Joe refuses each identity, but in the end he cannot escape being interpellated as a black killer of a white woman, an identity that in the racial ideology of his time and milieu dooms him.

Absalom, Absalom! (1936)

Faulkner often referred to *A Fable* as his "magnum o[pus]," his greatest work. Critical consensus awards that honor rather to *Absalom, Absalom!*, a novel of enormous scope and ambition and eloquence. *Absalom, Absalom!* presents Faulkner's definitive treatment of the myth of the South, but more than that it interrogates the very process of historical narrative and the elusive nature of truth.

Absalom, Absalom! marks a continuance of Faulkner's concerns in earlier novels. Not a sequel to *The Sound and the Fury*, *Absalom, Absalom!* does, however, return to the story of Quentin Compson and fills in gaps the earlier novel left unaddressed. The two novels are independent of one another and even contradict each other in small ways, but readers familiar with the Quentin of *The Sound and the Fury* will find subtexts in *Absalom, Absalom!* that echo Quentin's obsession with Caddy in the earlier work. The theme of miscegenation that resonates so powerfully in *Light in August* recurs here too.

SETTING

The primary settings of *Absalom, Absalom!* alternate between two days (one, in September 1909 in Jefferson, Mississippi, and the other in January 1910 in Cambridge, Massachusetts) and much of the nineteenth century, centered on Jefferson in the 1860s, the years before, during and after the Civil War. This dual framework of time and place sets up a contrast between the elusive historical past and a present-day vantage (1909–10) from which to interpret it. Furthermore, the contrast of the hot, dusty, wisteria-scented Mississippi September of the novel's present day (in the first half of the novel) with the snowy, iron-cold Massachusetts January of the second half also heightens the duality of the novel.

Some of the novel's past episodes range over settings that include Virginia and Haiti in the early nineteenth-century, the University of Mississippi in Oxford (40 miles from its fictional counterpart, Jefferson), the exotic New Orleans world of free people of color, and scattered scenes of Civil War military campaigns. The central setting of *Absalom, Absalom!* is Jefferson in Yoknapatawpha County, though, and the novel contributes an epic segment to Faulkner's fictional saga. There is even a link to the story of the Sartoris family. It is *Absalom's* Thomas Sutpen who replaced Col. Sartoris at the head of their Confederate regiment in the Civil War.

PLOT AND STRUCTURE

As in *The Sound and the Fury*, Faulkner builds *Absalom, Absalom!* around several characters' discourses about an absent central character's story. However, in *Absalom, Absalom!* he dramatizes the narration by providing detailed storytelling scenes and listeners for narrators' explicitly oral discourses, as opposed to revealing hidden streams of consciousness as in *The Sound and the Fury*. Some of the discourses retell stories handed down through the Compson family; key episodes are thus twice- and thrice-told tales. Faulkner further encloses and sometimes dissolves these oral accounts in an external narrative voice—distinctively Faulknerian—that constitutes an additional narrator's perspective.

The novel moves back and forth among pieces and versions of the story of the family of Thomas Sutpen (1807–69) and the attempts in 1909–10 to understand it by Quentin Compson, Sutpen's sister-in-law Rosa Coldfield, Quentin's father, and Quentin's roommate at Harvard, Shreve McCannon. Faulkner fragments and submerges the known facts of the Sutpens' story in a sea of speculation that colors and clouds them with the biases and obsessions of the narrators. Ultimately it is the interpretation of Sutpen's story by Quentin and Shreve that somewhat coalesces the novel's diffuseness. Like the plot of *Light in August*, that of *Absalom, Absalom!*, has elements of a detective story in which the motive of a murderer is the mystery, not his identity.

The narrators do not dispute the basic outline of Sutpen's story, although many details and the larger meanings are contested. What, then, is the basic story? Essentially, it was that "of a man who wanted a son through pride, and got too many of them and they destroyed him," as Faulkner wrote Harrison Smith in 1934 (Blotner, *Selected Letters* 84). The story began in 1833 when Thomas Sutpen arrived in Jefferson as a young man of 25 and by force of will and determination created a plantation and a dynasty. He acquired 100 square miles of land from the Chickasaw Indian chief Ikkemotubbe; then, with 20 Haitian slaves and a French architect, he built a splendid manor house on the estate he called Sutpen's Hundred. The next year, Sutpen produced a mulatto daughter named Clytie with a slave woman. Four years later he married Ellen Coldfield, the highly respectable daughter of a local merchant, and he soon produced a dynastic heir in his son Henry as well as a daughter Judith. Henry and Judith grew up with their half-sister Clytie as a servant in the household.

In 1859, Henry went to college at the nearby state university, where he became friends with Charles Bon, a sophisticate from New Orleans. Visiting Sutpen's Hundred on several occasions, Bon became unofficially engaged to Judith, but at Christmas in 1860 Henry quarreled with his father and disappeared with Bon, renouncing his birthright. The Civil War intervened, and the men were away fighting when Ellen died in 1863. Shortly after the end of the War, the crucial central action of the novel occurred when Henry killed Bon at the gates of Sutpen's Hundred and disappeared.

When the widowed Sutpen subsequently returned from the War to his impoverished plantation, he proposed marriage to his sister-in-law Rosa Coldfield but she broke off the engagement when Sutpen suggested she give him a son and heir as a pre-condition of their marriage. In 1867, Sutpen seduced Milly Jones, the granddaughter of Wash Jones, a hired hand who helped him run a small country store. When Milly gave birth to a girl and Sutpen rejected them, Jones killed Sutpen, Milly, and her baby.

The story of the House of Sutpen continues after Sutpen's death, though. In 1871, Charles Bon's 12-year-old son Charles Etienne de Saint Valery Bon (born in 1859 to Bon's octoroon mistress in New Orleans) came to live at Sutpen's Hundred, brought by Clytie at Judith's request. He subsequently married a black woman and their son Jim Bond was born in 1882. Two years later, Judith and Charles Etienne both died of yellow fever, leaving Clytie and Jim Bond remaining at Sutpen's Hundred.

When the novel opens in September 1909, Rosa Coldfield has summoned Quentin Compson just before he leaves for his first year at Harvard to tell him her version of Sutpen's story and for him to accompany her out to Sutpen's Hundred where, in the novel's shocking final revelation, they find the aged, decrepit Henry in hiding. The following December, Rosa went back to bring Henry to town, but he died along with Clytie when Clytie set fire to the house. Among the ruins of Sutpen's domain, only Jim Bond, a howling, slack-mouthed idiot, remained.

Complicating the issue of the authenticity of Sutpen's story as thus summarized, Faulkner's distillation of the so-called facts of the story in a Chronology and Genealogy appended to the novel contained details contradicted by the text of the novel. In his "corrected text" of 1986, Noel Polk reconciled these appendices with the novel. But many questions continue to be debated by critics.

Faulkner does not present the Sutpen story in such a linear, coherent form, though. He fragments the story into a crazy quilt of episodes and versions in a complex, deliberately disorienting manner. Michael Millgate provides a useful conception of the novel's convoluted structure:

> One way of looking at the book's structure is to think of it as organised about a number of crucial moments of recognition, truth, disillusion: Henry and his father [quarreling] in the library, Henry shooting Bon, Sutpen proposing to Rosa, Wash Jones murdering Sutpen—each moment presented in a kind of tableau arrested at a particular point in time and held in suspension while it is looked at, approached from all sides, inspected as if it were an artifact. . . . The main business of the book then becomes the interpretation of these moments, the attempt to explain and make sense of them. (*Achievement* 164)

The most pivotal questions of interpretation are why Sutpen forbids the marriage of Judith and Bon, and the reason Henry killed Bon four years later. Robert Dale Parker outlines four main explanations that the novel presents in a sequence of progressively mounting explanatory power.

First is Rosa's non-explanation: "I saw Judith's marriage forbidden without rhyme or reason or shadow of excuse" (12); much less did she understand why Henry killed Bon. Second, Mr. Compson assumed that Sutpen forbade Bon's marriage to Judith because of the threat of bigamy posed by Bon's previous (although unsanctioned) marriage to his octoroon mistress; Henry's loyalty to Bon then led him to deny his father's accusation and reject his birthright to go off with Bon. The reason for the killing, according to Mr. Compson, was that Henry, discovering the truth of his father's accusation, gave Bon four years to renounce his mistress and son. When Bon refused and returned to Sutpen's Hundred to marry Judith, Henry killed him. In a third explanation, Quentin reveals in chapter 7 that Bon was Sutpen's son by a previous marriage in Haiti, a detail that Quentin apparently only learned on the night in 1909 when he and Miss Rosa went out to Sutpen's Hundred and found Henry. Thus,

Henry's reason for killing Bon would have been to prevent incest between Judith and her half-brother. Finally, though, near the end of the novel, Quentin and Shreve somehow discover that Bon's mother in Haiti was part black, leaving the fear of miscegenation as the ultimate motive for Henry killing his half-brother and friend (Parker, *Absalom, Absalom! The Questioning of Fictions* 162–63).

Radically skeptical readings of the novel question the authenticity of—and even the possibility of knowing for sure—such crucial details as whether Charles Bon had any black blood or Sutpen was his father. Some critics (such as Robert Dale Parker in *Absalom, Absalom! The Questioning of Fictions*) infer that Quentin learns the facts of Bon's ancestry directly from Henry when he accompanies Rosa to the Sutpen mansion in September 1910: "Neither Faulkner, in his own or the novel's exterior narrative voice, nor any character ever says outright that Henry tells Quentin, but many critics, including this one, believe that Faulkner definitely though not clearly implies that Henry tells Quentin" (*Absalom, Absalom! The Questioning of Fictions* 139).

Donald Kartiganer, though, points out that it makes no sense for Quentin to develop with Shreve at such length the third explanation of the killing (as motivated by fear of incest) if he also learned about the miscegenation at the same time. He posits instead that it is only with Shreve's help that Quentin realizes the truth: "this last truth is something that Quentin can really *know*, can possess as a truth of the Sutpen family, only with the aid of Shreve and the communion that is created between them. Only then can he know what perhaps he has always known but could not admit to knowing, could not grasp except in the images of imaginatively realized truth" (Kartiganer 101).

Some of the critical controversy surrounding the novel stems from the ambiguous nature of the external narrative voice. Dirk Kuyk, Jr. argues that this external voice omnisciently confirms Quentin's claim that Bon was part black. However, Hugh Ruppersburg points out that the external narrator is "not omniscient—at least he does not exercise omniscience, often speaking in a conditional, speculative manner suggesting his uncertainty about, or unwillingness to divulge, the truth" (*Voice and Eye in Faulkner's Fiction* 95–96).

Whether authoritatively or not, the external narrator validates Quentin's and Shreve's intensely imagined account of the pivotal conversation between Henry and his father in 1864 in which Sutpen, as a last resort to prevent the marriage of Judith and Bon, plays his trump: the race card. The external narrator marks the transition to this key scene by stating that Quentin and Shreve through the power of their imagination merge with Henry and Bon and are thus somehow present at the scene in the Carolinas in 1864 late in the war when Sutpen arrives to confront his son. The shift to italic type signals Quentin's and Shreve's mystical movement back in time and space.

> Now neither of them was there [in Cambridge, Massachusetts in 1910]. They were both in Carolina and the time was forty-six years ago, and it was not even four now but compounded still further, since now both of them were Henry Sutpen and both of them were Bon, compounded each of both yet either neither, smelling the very smoke which had blown and faded away forty-six years ago from the *bivouac fires burning in a pine grove.* (280)

Thus commences a six-page passage in italics that includes Sutpen's telling Henry that Bon must not marry Judith because "after he [Bon] was born . . . I found out that his mother was part negro" (283) and the subsequent confrontation in which Bon tells Henry "So it's the miscegenation, not the incest, which you cant bear":

> —You shall not.
> —Who will stop me, Henry?
> —No, Henry says.—No. No. No.
> Now it is Bon who watches Henry. . . . His hand vanishes beneath the blanket and reappears, holding his pistol by the barrel, the butt extended toward Henry.
> —Then do it now, he says.
> Henry looks at the pistol; now he is not only panting, he is trembling; when he speaks now his voice is not even the exhalation, it is the suffused and suffocating inbreath itself:
> —You are my brother.
> —No I'm not. I'm the nigger that's going to sleep with your sister. Unless you stop me, Henry. (285–86)

Here is the novel's ultimate explanation for the fratricide that is the crux of the plot.

Faulkner builds suspense by presenting the previous explanations as red herrings that each give way to subsequent explanations. He further heightens the suspense with cliff-hanging endings to key chapters. The first five chapters of the novel are set in 1909 on the long September day leading into night when Quentin listens to Miss Rosa and then his father tell their versions of Sutpen's story. Chapter 1, the introduction of Rosa's version, ends with Rosa's implicit revelation of Clytie's parentage. Chapters 2 through 4 present Mr. Compson's interpretation of the story, based on what he was told by his father Gen. Compson, Sutpen's only friend and confidant, and chapter 5 returns to Rosa's account from earlier in the day. Chapters 3, 4, and 5 all end by circling back to Henry's shooting of Bon, each time providing more information. Chapter 5 adds a further chill of suspense when Rosa tells Quentin in 1909 that "There's something in that house. . . . Something living in it. Hidden in it. It has been out there for four years, living hidden in that house" (140).

The remaining four chapters of the novel move to Quentin and Shreve's dormitory room at Harvard in January 1910, as they obsessively try to assemble and make sense of Sutpen's story. Chapter 6 ends with Quentin on the verge of revealing to Shreve what he and Rosa found that September night at Sutpen's Hundred. Chapter 7 ends with an account of another murder—Jones killing Sutpen with a rusty scythe. The tension mounts further in chapter 8 as Quentin and Shreve seem to travel back in time and witness the scenes that finally explain Henry's murder of Bon. In the last chapter of the novel, in their cold, dark dorm room after midnight, Quentin remembers his nightmarish journey with Miss Rosa to Sutpen's Hundred three months earlier.

CHARACTERS

Thomas Sutpen

Thomas Sutpen is a larger-than-life character that looms over the world of *Absalom, Absalom!* like a figure out of myth or legend but one that the narrators each characterize according to her or his own need. A demon to Miss Rosa and akin to a figure out of Greek tragedy to Quentin's father, Sutpen revealed himself to Quentin's grandfather as an innocent scarred for life in adolescence. The traumatic formative event occurred when a rich man's house slave, treating him like white trash, turned him away from the front door of the man's Tidewater Virginia mansion. The shock of that rejection at age 14 motivated Sutpen to revenge himself by acquiring wealth and slaves and an estate of his own. With single-minded purpose, knowing he possessed the necessary courage and believing he could learn the requisite shrewdness, he formed a plan he called his "design." Faulkner leaves the precise nature of Sutpen's design only implied. Presumably it entailed not only material wealth and property but also the founding of a dynasty to inherit it.

He first attempted to enact his design in Haiti where he worked as the overseer of a Frenchman's sugar plantation. In gratitude for Sutpen quelling a slave rebellion, the owner of the plantation gave his daughter to Sutpen in marriage. When a child was born, though, Sutpen rejected his wife and son as not "adjunctive" to his design in an ironic repetition of his own rejection at 14.

The second attempt to make his design a reality resulted in Sutpen's Hundred, his marriage to Ellen Coldfield, and the births of Henry and Judith. The arrival of Charles Bon at Sutpen's Hundred as a suitor for Judith, though, set in motion a series of events that disrupted the design again by removing the dynastic heir. Like Sutpen himself as a youth, Bon was in effect turned away from the door of a great house, in another ironic repetition.

Nearing sixty and with time running out, Sutpen proposed to his sister-in-law Rosa that she produce a male heir as a prerequisite for marriage. When Rosa was outraged by his proposition, he seduced Milly Jones in an effort to produce a male heir but the design failed a third time when her child turned out to be a girl. Sutpen's final attempt to complete his design ended in Milly's grandfather revenging Sutpen's rejection of them by killing him with a scythe.

As a determined but unscrupulous self-made man, Sutpen embodies the dark side of the American Dream and is thus kin to F. Scott Fitzgerald's Jay Gatsby, whose obsession with wealth also ends in death. Sutpen's doom links him specifically to the South, though, in that it stems from the curse of slavery. Sutpen is too much of a nouveau riche outsider in Jefferson society to be as representative of the Old South as Col. Sartoris, but the fate of the House of Sutpen echoes that of the South. By siring both black and white sons and rejecting his black son, he plants the seeds of the destruction of his design.

Sutpen defies racist stereotypes in some ways, though. He pays his wild Haitian slaves the respect of wrestling with them on equal terms in the "raree shows" he puts on to entertain the men of Jefferson, and during Reconstruction he refuses to join his neighbors in terrorizing free blacks. He betrays racial prejudice with tragic consequence, however, in rejecting his first wife presumably for the taint of black blood and then repudiating their son Charles. His children suffer the consequences of these mistakes and inherit a tragic legacy.

Sutpen's Children

Thomas Sutpen had five children by four different women, and race and gender played determining roles in their lives. In the patriarchal, racially divided society of the South in the nineteenth century, only white male children figured as significant elements in the design Sutpen envisioned. His daughter Judith functions in this patriarchal design only as a token of exchange in the relations between men, while his daughter Clytie (born to an unnamed slave woman) figures not at all in the design. His daughter by Milly Jones is killed shortly after her birth and thus also plays no role. In shaping his novel *Absalom, Absalom!*, though, Faulkner arranges these characters as well as Henry and Bon into designs that undermine and critique Sutpen's.

Henry, Judith, and Charles

Early in the novel, Rosa contrasts the different ways the children raised at Sutpen's Hundred respond to the brutal wrestling match in the barn between their father and one of his slaves. Henry, sickened by the violence, screams and vomits while Judith and Clytie, hidden in the loft, watch impassively. Behaving counter to gender stereotypes, Henry betrays a feminine sensitivity and Judith and Clytie reveal a masculine stoicism that characterizes them as adults as well, even as Rosa emphasizes the difference in the color of their "two Sutpen faces" (22).

Henry and Judith are often paired in the design of the novel. Mr. Compson reports that "between Judith and Henry there had been a relationship closer than the traditional loyalty of brother and sister even" (62). He attributes to them a "telepathy with which as children they seemed at times to anticipate one another's actions" such that "it must have been Henry who seduced Judith, not Bon" into their presumed engagement (79), thus arranging by proxy a figuratively "pure and perfect incest" between Henry and Judith (77). The introduction of Bon into the relationship between Judith and Henry triangulated the brother-sister pair into a three-way incestuous grouping.

At the University of Mississippi, Henry had met and quickly became infatuated with the worldly Charles Bon, imitating his elegant manners and dress. Raised in rural northern Mississippi, Henry was provincial and immature whereas Charles, eight years older, was a product of sophisticated, sensual New Orleans society. Mr. Compson describes Charles "as a sort of Creole roué" (Ruppersburg 91), exotically feminine and catlike, who seduced Henry and (through him) Judith both into loving him (74–76). When Quentin reveals Sutpen's confession that Bon is also his son, the relationship between all three siblings takes on explicitly incestuous overtones.

Henry's bond with Charles is so close that he renounces his birthright and goes off with him, first to New Orleans and eventually as soldiers together in the same Confederate company. In New Orleans, Bon introduces Henry to his octoroon mistress, which Mr. Compson initially believes accounts for Henry killing Bon to prevent his marriage to Judith. In Shreve and Quentin's account, Bon rescues the wounded Henry at the battle of Pittsburgh Landing (also known as the battle of Shiloh), and Henry struggles to overcome his objections to Bon marrying Judith. The octoroon mistress and even incest he can accept, but not Bon's black blood.

Shreve's (and Quentin's) account of Bon's motives is complex and suggests Shreve's close identification with Bon, a reflection of their shared status as Yoknapatawpha outsiders, Shreve being Canadian and Bon, a French-speaking New Orleansian. Out of his youthful romanticism, Shreve asserts that, as opposed to seeking revenge or blackmail, Bon loved Judith and wanted his father to acknowledge him as a son. Shreve quotes Bon as saying to Henry, "But he [Sutpen] didn't [acknowledge me]. If he had, I would have agreed and promised never to see her or you or him again. . . . He just told you, sent me a message like you send a command by a nigger servant to a beggar or a tramp to clear out" (272). Bon's analogy also ironically mirrors Sutpen's literal experience as a youth in Virginia. To Shreve, Bon is a romantic figure, not a villain exploiting his parentage. Adelaide McGinnis states that "Bon embodies the dark, natural sensuality that is necessary for wholeness as a human being. . . . [He] is not the villain of *Absalom, Absalom!* . . . Rather, he is the would-be emancipator of Henry" (225–26).

Judith and Clytie

Judith Sutpen rose above the limitations of her social role as a Southern belle and displayed tremendous stoicism at Sutpen's Hundred during and after the War. She endured the deaths of her mother, her intended husband, and her father, and she took in Bon's son Charles Etienne. In spite of these adversities, she remained inscrutable and somewhat cold. Her few tears over Bon's death when she greeted her father months later were brief. "Judith is doomed by misfortunes not of her making," Cleanth Brooks observes, "but she is not warped and twisted by them. Her humanity survives them" (*William Faulkner: The Yoknapatawpha Country* 319).

In her hardships, Judith is paired with her black half-sister Clytie. Thadious Davis comments that "Clytie, as black twin to Judith, becomes a subtle statement of the oneness of humankind. The common bonds of temperament, interests, duty, and affection unite the two women in a sisterhood that transcends race" (*Faulkner's "Negro"* 201). Unlike Dilsey in *The Sound and the Fury*, Clytie lacked the comforts of the black church, community, and even family. As a half-black daughter of her father, she both was and was not a Sutpen, but she slept beside Judith on a pallet and worked beside her to sustain life at Sutpen's Hundred.

Clytie is dramatically contrasted, on the other hand, with Rosa Coldfield on two occasions when Rosa attempted to pass Clytie to go upstairs at Sutpen's Hundred. The first time, when Henry has killed Bon, Clytie defied custom by taking hold of Rosa's arm and addressing her familiarly as Rosa rather than Miss Rosa: *"Dont you go up there, Rosa"* (111). Despite acknowledging to herself that they are "twin sistered to a fell darkness which had produced her," Rosa responds *"Take your hand off me, nigger!"* (112). Thadious Davis points out that "Rosa's meeting with Clytie is a central scene because it reverberates all the tensions between black and white, between classes and races that have been used to define the South and to establish the major concerns of the novel. One of the most starkly honest scenes in the Faulkner canon, this meeting probes the psychological and cultural realities of race and kinship" (207). Furthermore, "it is a tableau extending Sutpen's treatment of his son Charles Bon to the conduct of an entire society" (Davis, *Faulkner's "Negro"* 210).

A parallel scene occurs 45 years later, when Rosa comes out to Sutpen's Hundred with Quentin. This time, Rosa knocks Clytie down and ascends the stairs to find Henry hiding upstairs. In the final pairing of Sutpen's children in the novel, Clytie is linked with Henry, hiding and protecting him from retribution for killing Bon. She even chooses to die with her half-brother by setting fire to the house.

THE NARRATOR/CHARACTERS

Rosa Coldfield

Rosa's direct knowledge of the Sutpen family privileges her present-day narrative as uniquely first-hand, even as her sense of outrage distorts it. In her "grim haggard amazed voice" (3), Rosa narrates how her future brother-in-law Thomas Sutpen "tore violently a plantation" from land 12 miles northwest of Jefferson (5). Rosa was born four years after her niece Judith and thus only had opportunity to observe him after he had established Sutpen's Hundred, and her account of him is far from objective. Traumatized at 20 by his outrageous proposal to bear him a son before marriage, Rosa voices her impotent rage at him by characterizing him as an ogre and a demon.

The external narrator describes the 64-year-old Rosa as a "crucified child" (4), sitting stiffly in a straight-backed chair "so tall for her that her legs hung straight and rigid as if she had iron shinbones and ankles, clear of the floor with that air of impotent and static rage like children's feet" (3). Her childish appearance is ironic in that she had grown up without experiencing childhood. Born late in life to her father Goodhue Coldfield, Rosa never knew her mother, who died giving birth to her. Forced by the age of 10 to keep house for her father, she was a teenager during the Civil War, during which her sister died (after charging Rosa to look after Judith) and her father in protest of the War boarded himself up in the attic and also died. In 1865, at the age of 20, after her nephew Henry killed Charles Bon, Rosa moved to Sutpen's Hundred where she lived until her brother-in-law returned from the War and they became engaged. His outrageous proposition three months later drove her back to the Coldfield house in Jefferson where, 43 years later, she summoned Quentin Compson to hear her story.

Long silent (although established as the county's poetess laureate for her eulogies in the newspaper to the undefeated spirit of the South), she vents to Quentin in a voice of "incredulous and unbearable amazement" her shock and outrage at Sutpen's 43-year-old insult, "the old unforgiving outraged and betrayed by the final and complete affront which was Sutpen's death" (9). In addition to venting her long pent-up rage to Quentin, chosen apparently because he is the grandson of Sutpen's only friend, Rosa also demands that he take her after dark out to Sutpen's Hundred where she believes someone is hiding—her nephew Henry, in fact.

Linda Wagner-Martin emphasizes that Rosa's pain and grief stem not only from Sutpen's treatment of her, but also from her father's neglect. Repeatedly left standing outside closed doors, Rosa "has no house, no door, no physical location except that of her imagination and her narrative" (Wagner-Martin "Rosa Coldfield as Daughter" 232). The repeated image of Rosa shut out by a closed door (such as when her father nails himself behind the attic door and when Clytie and Judith refuse to admit her to the room where Bon lies dead) "is an ironic echo of Sutpen's compelling 'door' narrative, when he is stigmatized by being sent around to the back, by a black, and refused entrance through a front door" (232).

Mr. Compson

Unlike Rosa's first-hand account of Sutpen, Mr. Compson (Jason Compson III) receives his second-hand from his father, Gen. Jason Compson II. Furthermore, in the second half of the novel, this second-hand account is filtered third-hand by Quentin to Shreve. "Mr. Compson's narrative of the Sutpen history," Donald Kartiganer notes, "appears to stand in relationship to Miss Rosa's as a cool, rationalistic version to a near-hysterical one. Yet we must not infer from this a genuine objectivity or disinterest: just as much as Rosa, Compson creates his tale out of his own psychic and emotional needs" (Kartiganer 76). Mr. Compson assumes an air of detachment, even cynicism, in his view of the Sutpen story, describing them as victims of fate similar to the characters in Greek tragedy. He sees the Sutpens as capable of gigantic actions because they are simpler and less complex than someone of his superior twentieth-century intellect. In this way, Kartiganer explains, he indirectly excuses his own inaction, frustration, and defeat, detailed in *The Sound and the Fury* but implicit in *Absalom, Absalom!* (Kartiganer 76–79).

Just as Rosa is obsessed with Thomas Sutpen, the demon lover who was her only chance for a husband and family, Mr. Compson is fascinated with Charles Bon. He projects on to Bon an "air of sardonic and indolent detachment" out of his own detached cynicism (74). Much of Mr. Compson's account of Bon is imagined or intuited. It is Mr. Compson who sees Henry as infatuated with Bon to the point that he engineers an engagement between him and Judith. Mr. Compson is too cynical to think that Bon loved Judith.

Yet Mr. Compson admits that his theory that Henry killed Bon because of Bon's connection to the octoroon mistress "does not explain . . . and we are not supposed to know" (80). Ultimately, Mr. Compson falls back on fate as "the basis of [his] understanding of the Sutpen story, and Charles Bon becomes the key to his narrative because Bon is the complete fatalist" (Kartiganer 86). Mr. Compson accepts meaningless fate as the explanation that "does not explain" because it excuses his own passivity and cynicism.

Quentin and Shreve

Quentin Compson and his Canadian roommate at Harvard, Shreve McCannon, learn from Mr. Compson in a letter in January 1910 that Miss Rosa has died. This prompts them to sift through the unexplained Sutpen saga yet again. Shreve's initial flippant summary of the story sarcastically refers to Rosa as "this old dame" and Sutpen as a Faustus and a Beelzebub, but the focus shifts in chapter 6 to a serious account of Charles Etienne (filtered mostly through Mr. Compson) and in chapter 7 to Sutpen's own account of his life as told to Gen. Compson on two occasions 30 years apart and retold by Mr. Compson to Quentin.

In the middle of chapter 7, though, Shreve abruptly interrupts Quentin's summary of Sutpen's account to Gen. Compson of how he paid off and abandoned his first wife and son. Introducing the idea that Sutpen is Bon's father, Shreve says "So that Christmas Henry brought him [Bon] home, into the house, and the demon looked up and saw the face he believed he had paid off and discharged twenty-eight years ago" (213). More surprisingly, though, Quentin reveals "Grandfather didn't tell [Father] all of it either, like Sutpen never told Grandfather quite all of it" (214). Rather,

Quentin himself told his father this part of the story that Quentin only learned "that night when we—" (meaning when Miss Rosa and Quentin went out to Sutpen's Hundred in September 1909). From this point, Quentin and Shreve are actively narrating their own versions of the story.

Their first version, with incest at the heart of it, is romantic and Byronic, a tale filtered through their own youthful identification with Henry and Bon as alter egos. This version, as Donald Kartiganer puts it, is "a story of love and youthful heroism, intensified because it is also a story of potential incest" (94). Yet this version also fails to explain the killing when Shreve and Quentin jointly realize that Henry was willing to accept incest between Judith and Bon—until, that is, they uncover the truth of Bon's black blood. "The invention of Bon's Negro blood," according to Kartiganer, "is the great imaginative leap of the novel, and it comes about primarily because of what has been happening to Quentin and Shreve during the bulk of their narration: the growing sense of communion, of the created tale as a . . . marriage of minds" (98). He quotes the external narrator: "it did not matter to either of them which one did the talking, since it was not the talking alone which did it . . . but some happy marriage of speaking and hearing wherein each before the demand, the requirement, forgave condoned and forgot the faulting of the other" (253). Kartiganer sees this part of the novel as "the climactic moment in Faulkner's career, for it is here that his essential style of fragmentation, of isolated narrators and actors placed at odd intervals on the rim of a single event, moves toward its most profound meaning" (92).

In a famous psychological interpretation of *Absalom, Absalom!* considered alongside *The Sound and the Fury*, John T. Irwin argues that Henry and Bon represent two opposed sides of Quentin's psyche. Henry represents the part of him that sees himself as an idealized protector of a sister's honor, whereas Bon functions as Quentin's shadow, whose black blood threatens both incest and death. Thus Bon's killing of Henry foreshadows Quentin's suicide in *The Sound and the Fury*. Conflating the two novels' Quentins into a single character, however, is fraught with difficulties, the least of which is that Shreve's last name is different in the two novels and Caddy is never mentioned in *Absalom, Absalom!* The recurrence of the incest theme in the minds of both Quentins, though, provides a striking extratextual subtext for *Absalom, Absalom!*

THEMES

Among many themes in *Absalom, Absalom!* two major ones are the impact of the abstract idea of the Negro in the South and the unknowability of truth. In regard to the former theme, Thadious Davis declares that "a black presence dominates this work as it does perhaps no other Faulkner novel. Nowhere else is it so apparent that the Negro is an abstract force confounding southern life both past and present even while, paradoxically, stimulating much of that life and art" (*Faulkner's "Negro"* 181). Davis points out that Thomas Sutpen formulates his grand design in reaction to being turned away from a plantation's big house by a Negro house slave to whom Sutpen refers as the "monkey nigger." "In closing the door, the 'monkey nigger' opened the boy Sutpen to a painful awareness of the inner dynamics of southern life. Because of his action, the 'monkey nigger' balloons up larger than life; he becomes at once a visible metaphor for social reality and an allusive, invisible presence in the boy's life" (*Faulkner's "Negro"* 184). Furthermore, each of the narrators of Sutpen's story invents

> his own "Negro" in defining himself and in expressing the limits of his imagination, personality, and humanity. Miss Rosa creates Clytie, Sutpen's slave daughter, and the 'wild niggers' who build Sutpen's Hundred. Mr. Compson draws the New Orleans octoroon and her son Charles Etienne St. Valery Bon. Quentin and Shreve imagine Charles Bon and his mother Eulalia. . . . All of their projections operate to enrich the significance of "Negro" as both abstraction and metaphorical reality in *Absalom, Absalom!* (189–90).

The novel's convoluted form and its famous difficulty for readers are intrinsic to the second theme of the unknowability of truth. *Absalom, Absalom!* challenges readers to join Miss Rosa, Mr. Compson, Quentin, Shreve, and the external narrator to craft their own version of the story of Thomas Sutpen and his children. When asked if any of the narrators has the "right view, or is it more or less a case of thirteen ways of looking at a blackbird [an allusion to a poem by Wallace Stevens] with none of them right?" Faulkner responded:

> That's it exactly. I think that no one individual can look at truth. It blinds you. You look at it and you see one phase of it. Someone else looks at it and sees a slightly awry phase of it. But taken all together, the truth is in what they saw though nobody saw the truth intact. So these are true as far as Miss Rosa and Quentin saw it. Quentin's father saw what he believed was truth, that was all he saw. But the old man was himself a little too big for people no greater in stature than Quentin and Miss Rosa and Mr. Compson to see all at once. It would have taken perhaps a wiser or more tolerant or more sensitive or more thoughtful person to see him as he was. It was, as you say, thirteen ways of looking at a blackbird. But the truth, I would like to think, comes out, that when the reader has read all these thirteen different ways of looking at the blackbird, the reader has his own fourteenth

image of that blackbird which I would like to think is the truth. (Gwynn and Blotner 273–74)

SYMBOLS AND ALLUSIONS

Faulkner's title alludes to the biblical story in 2 Samuel of the sons of King David by different wives, Absalom and Amnon. When Amnon rapes their sister Tamar, Absalom has him killed and flees into exile. Absalom later dies rebelling against his father, and David laments "O my son Absalom, my son, my son Absalom!" (2 Samuel 18:33). Although the brother-sister incest in the novel *Absalom, Absalom!* is only threatened, the biblical motifs of fratricide and exile recur in both works.

Faulkner also frequently alludes to the Trojan War in *Absalom, Absalom!* Clytie's name is short for Clytemnestra, the wife of Agamemnon who murdered him in retaliation for the sacrificial death of their daughter Iphigenia. Mr. Compson suggests that perhaps Sutpen was thinking instead of Cassandra, the daughter of Troy who prophesied its fall. Several times in the novel, Rosa Coldfield is associated with Cassandra's powers of unheeded prophecy.

As with *Light in August,* Faulkner again used the working title "Dark House," suggesting allusions to the Gothic novel tradition, including the novels *Jane Eyre* and *Wuthering Heights* by Charlotte and Emily Brontë, respectively. Sutpen's rejected Haitian wife is reminiscent of Rochester's first wife in the former novel and both novels end with the burning of great houses. Rosa's demonization of Sutpen recalls Nelly Dean's characterization of Heathcliff in *Wuthering Heights; Absalom, Absalom!* also shares with that novel a complex layering of narrative voices and the stretching of the story across several generations of linked families.

In the American novelistic tradition, the Southern curse of slavery in *Absalom, Absalom!* parallels the Northern curse of Puritanism in Hawthorne's fiction, and Sutpen's egomania is reminiscent of Ahab's in Melville's *Moby-Dick.* Faulkner's network of allusions and intertextual references in *Absalom, Absalom!* is wide-ranging and suggests his ambition that the novel be compared with the greatest achievements in American literature. Shortly after completing it, he told a colleague in Hollywood "I think it's the best novel yet written by an American" (Blotner, *Faulkner* 364).

ALTERNATIVE READING: HISTORICIST

Historicist literary critics examine literary texts in their historical contexts, as opposed examining them as formal aesthetic objects detached from the circumstances of their production. A historicist reading is particularly appropriate to a text such as *Absalom, Absalom!* that is itself very much about the process of historical investigation. Simon Malpas explains that "For the historicist critic . . . there are not eternal meanings or truths that exist entirely outside the processes of historical change: all meaning is historically mutable because it is situated in and generated by its context" (58). Just as the lives of Rosa, Mr. Compson, Quentin and Shreve affect their understanding of the truth of Thomas Sutpen's life, historicist readers of *Absalom, Absalom!* acknowledge the contingent nature of their own readings of the novel.

Influenced by the theories of Michel Foucault, historicist critics recognize that conflicting interests and discourses compete to shape the way groups are identified in categories such as criminal, insane, or sexually deviant in given historical periods. Rather than attributing such identities to natural or divine forces, historicists following Foucault look to the exercise of power as the source of such labels. The aim of Foucault's work and historicist critics in his mold is "to carefully disentangle the myriad ways in which power is produced and organized in a society or period, how it circulates in that culture to generate particular identities and institutions, and how alternative ways of thinking and being, resistances, might be made available" (Malpas 61).

In *Absalom, Absalom!* Southern society uses all the force of law and custom to impose on characters with black blood the identity of "nigger" with disastrous results for the House of Sutpen. An historicist reading of the novel reveals the context from which this stigmatized identity emerged, including some details of Faulkner's family history that enrich our understanding of the Sutpens.

Historian Joel Williamson describes the phenomenon of "shadow families" in the South, occurring when a man "reared a mulatto family in the servant's quarters at the very same time that he maintained a white family in the main house, in effect having two wives simultaneously. Ironically, the mulatto family sometimes mirrored the white family not only woman for woman, but child for child, and, because it lived in the very shadow of the white family, might well be called the 'shadow family'" (25). Williamson documents evidence that Faulkner's great-grandfather William C. Falkner fathered such a shadow family and supported them for many years.

The historical record also shows, according to Williamson, that in the Southern social world, "forms were not always pure and some transgressions were tolerated—even if grudgingly so," leading him to conclude that "In real life, almost surely, Thomas Sutpen could have publicly recognized Charles Bon as his son and had the essence of his

Grand Design too. In the real world, Bon could have married white and eventually graced Sutpen's Hundred as its master" (384). This historical perspective illuminates the distinctiveness of Sutpen's design and his rigidity in pursuing it. If Williamson's analysis begs the question of the incestuous implications of Bon marrying Judith, his half-sister, it does challenge the assumption that Bon's drop of black blood disqualified him for Sutpen's recognition as his son and heir.

Williamson's research also sheds light on Clytie's role in the Sutpen family, explaining the tacit acceptance of her as a shadow Sutpen, and on Judith's acceptance of Charles Etienne. She took him in (presumably never realizing that he was her nephew) and gave him a trundle bed between her and Clytie. In this act, she rose above the racism to which her father succumbed and resisted the power structure that defined Charles Etienne as a so-called nigger. Thus the novel poses an alternative to the dominant power structure and how it defines identities.

8

Short Fiction

In the course of his career, William Faulkner wrote about 120 short stories (Skei 6). Although he occasionally claimed that he ranked short stories second only to poetry in the hierarchy of literary genres, he wrote most of his stories when he was in financial difficulties as a way to make money. When he married in 1929 and bought Rowan Oak the next year, he started publishing stories in national magazines, the first being "A Rose for Emily" in *Forum* in April 1930. The most lucrative venues for stories at that time were mass-market magazines such as *The Saturday Evening Post*, which paid him as much as $1,000 for stories, so Faulkner tried to write stories that would appeal to the *Post*'s editors. He succeeded early on with "Thrift," "Red Leaves," and "Lizards in Jamshyd's Court-yard," for the latter two of which he received $750 each in 1931. The *Post* paid Faulkner more for four stories than he had received for his first four novels (Karl 401). In 1931, Faulkner published *These 13*, a collection of stories that sold more than any of his previous books, with the exception of *Sanctuary*. Another collection, entitled *Dr. Martino and Other Stories*, appeared in 1934.

In 1932, Faulkner changed his money-making strategy from magazines to movies and his production of short stories alternated throughout the 1930s with lucrative stints in Hollywood. Faulkner viewed these income streams as necessary to support what he considered his serious writing of novels, yet stories such as "Barn Burning" are masterpieces of the form. In

1950, Faulkner published 42 stories as his *Collected Stories*, and, in 1979, Joseph Blotner edited and published another 45 *Uncollected Stories*.

Faulkner's short fiction is sometimes closely related to his novels. Several times Faulkner published linked collections of stories that approach the unity and shape of novels, many of which had been separately published in magazines, such as *The Unvanquished* in 1938 (as discussed in chapter 3) and *Knight's Gambit* in 1949. One such book, *Go Down, Moses* (1942), which includes *The Bear*, Faulkner considered a novel and was disconcerted when Random House initially published it under the title *Go Down, Moses and Other Stories*. Furthermore, some of his stories were later incorporated into novels in revised form (such as *Spotted Horses* and "Barn Burning" in *The Hamlet*) or treated characters from the novels (in the way "That Evening Sun" considers the Compson siblings as small children). Three longer works were published as *Three Famous Short Novels* in 1958: *Spotted Horses*, *Old Man*, and *The Bear*. Each work is also part of a larger novel, but by publishing them in this way as well, Faulkner's publisher Random House sanctioned reading them as autonomous works separate from the novels.

Faulkner's short fiction can be categorized in a variety of ways. This chapter examines a representative sampling, in the order of their publication, of fictional works of various lengths and types that Faulkner adapted for his own ends, such as war stories, detective stories, tall tales, gothic tales, and tales of adventure. In his *Collected Stories*, Faulkner himself grouped 42 of his stories into six vaguely geographical clusters that included "The Country," "The Village," "The Wilderness," "The Wasteland" (stories of World War I, the section name alluding to T. S. Eliot's poem), "The Middle Ground" (a somewhat miscellaneous category), and "Beyond." Edmond L. Volpe adopts and extends these groupings in his study of Faulkner's short fiction.

"A ROSE FOR EMILY" (1930)

"A Rose for Emily," Faulkner's most widely anthologized story, was the first one that Faulkner published in a national magazine. It was collected in *These 13* (1931) and in *Collected Stories* in the "Village" grouping (along with other stories set in the town of Jefferson), as well as in other collections of Faulkner's work. Couched as a memorial to Miss Emily Grierson, a reclusive spinster, the story carefully withholds information and manipulates time to build up to a shocking conclusion. The story contains such elements of gothic horror as a decaying mansion holding a horrific secret, but it moves beyond such easy classification by the adroitness of its handling of point of view and structure.

Setting

The story is set in Faulkner's fictional Jefferson, Mississippi, in a present time that is presumably not long before the story's publication date in 1930. In a series of flashbacks, the narrator establishes that the Griersons were an old, "high and mighty" aristocratic family, of which Miss Emily was the remnant. The townspeople regarded her as "a tradition, a duty, and a care; a sort of hereditary obligation on the town" (*Collected Stories* 119). They stood in awe of her patrician status even as they resented her haughtiness and pride. The lone survivor of her family and constrained by her class and gender from having a career, Miss Emily descended into genteel poverty but remained an aloof subject of town gossip.

Point of View and Structure

The narrator of "A Rose for Emily" is a plural first-person collective—*we*—who represents the townspeople of Jefferson. The narrator begins at the end, with the death of Miss Emily, and fills in a series of episodes in the town's interactions with her over many years. These include her imperious claim that she was not subject to paying taxes and a time 30 years earlier when the town fathers were compelled to eliminate a foul smell coming from her house by sprinkling lime around the foundation.

The narrator skips to a brief account of Emily's overbearing father and how he pridefully prevented her from marrying while she still had the chance. At his death, Emily refused to accept it at first, a foreshadowing of greater instability to come. In the third of the story's five sections, the narrator describes the town's disapproving gossip at Emily taking up with a Yankee construction foreman named Homer Barron. When she purchased arsenic from a drugstore, "we all said, 'She will kill herself'" (*Collected Stories* 126), the narrator reports. However, speculation shifts to an anticipated wedding between Miss Emily and Homer Barron, until Homer disappears and Emily goes into deeper seclusion, her hair turning a "vigorous iron-gray, like the hair of an active man" (*Collected Stories* 128).

The final section of the story narrates the funeral of Miss Emily and the opening of a room upstairs in her house. There the townspeople find, in a dusty bridal chamber, the decayed corpse of Homer Barron. In the pillow beside the body, they find "a long strand of iron-gray hair" (130), implying that Miss Emily had continued to sleep beside the long-dead corpse.

Characters, Themes, and Symbols

Like *Sanctuary*, "A Rose for Emily" has sensational elements (murder, necrophilia) that contributed to Faulkner's early reputation as a member of a literary "cult of cruelty." The sensationalism in "A Rose for Emily," though, is only revealed in the shocking conclusion of the story, allowing Faulkner first to characterize Emily Grierson as a complex figure. Herself a victim of sexual repression and stultifying gender roles, Emily is driven to insanity and murder by family and social dynamics. "'A Rose for Emily' is, among other things," according to James B. Carothers, "an expression of moral outrage, an indictment of those conventions and customs which drive Miss Emily to murder Homer Barron" (22).

Miss Emily is also a symbol of death-in-life and thus of the South's refusal to let die the myth of the Lost Cause. Looking in old age "like a body long submerged in motionless water" (*Collected Stories* 121), Miss Emily is a veritable monument to the Old South. Her house's "stubborn and coquettish decay" serves as a reminder of a way of life that is dead but unburied. When her father dies, she at first denies it, a presage of her later inability to let go of Homer Barron, even after his death. "A Rose for Emily" is a story that functions as both a thriller and an allegory.

"THAT EVENING SUN" (1931)

H. L. Mencken published "That Evening Sun" in *American Mercury* in March 1931, and Faulkner later published a slightly revised version in *These 13* and *Collected Stories*. Widely anthologized, "That Evening Sun" tells an episode in the lives of *The Sound and the Fury*'s Compson family involving a black laundress and cook named Nancy, a character who reappears in *Requiem for a Nun* (1951). Tautly suspenseful yet highly unresolved, the story has generated controversy among critics as to its meaning.

Setting and Point of View

Set in Jefferson, "That Evening Sun" is narrated by Quentin Compson at the age of 24, even though he died in *The Sound and the Fury* at the age of 20 in 1910. Faulkner shrugged off such discrepancies between his works with recurring characters by saying that his fictive world was alive and continued to grow and change as he returned to it (Cowley, *Faulkner-Cowley File* 90). "What we find in Faulkner's best fiction is the forceful expression of a comprehensive and generally coherent intelligence," James B. Carothers argues, "but each story or novel constitutes a different expression and implies a different intelligence" (13). Carothers thus suggests that we read "That Evening Sun" as autonomous from *The Sound and the Fury*, but still part of the Yoknapatawpha "mythology."

At the age of 24, then, Quentin looks back to a time 15 years earlier when he was nine, his sister Caddy was seven, and his brother Jason was five. (Benjy is not mentioned in the story.) Quentin mostly limits his narration to what his nine-year-old self perceived and understood. In this way, the point of view of the story creates a powerful tension between Nancy's adult world and the children's limited but growing understanding of it.

Plot and Structure

In the first of the story's six sections, Quentin introduces Nancy as a local laundress who cooks for the Compsons when their regular cook Dilsey is sick. Often late for work, Nancy is variously rumored to be a drunk, a cocaine addict, and a prostitute, although Quentin only reports with any certainty that, one time when she was under arrest and on her way to jail, she passed a Mr. Stovall on the street and accused him of not paying her. Even though he kicks her in the mouth, she continues to taunt him, saying "It's been three times now since he paid me a cent" (291). In jail and presumably pregnant, Nancy tries unsuccessfully to hang herself.

In a passage that Mencken asked Faulkner to cut when the story was originally published, Nancy taunts her husband Jesus in front of the Compson children by saying that the "watermelon" under her dress "never come off of your vine" (292). The implication is clearly that Nancy is pregnant by Mr. Stovall, and she fears that Jesus will murder her for cuckolding him. The remainder of the story traces Nancy's growing terror of Jesus and her attempts to use the Compson children as a shield against him. In the climactic episode, Nancy tries to distract the children in her cabin at night with stories and popcorn to keep them from leaving her alone. When Mr. Compson arrives to take the children home, Nancy resigns herself to her fate: "When yawl walk out that door, I gone" (307). The story ends without revealing what happens to Nancy, leading some readers to assume Nancy was wrong about the danger she sensed and others to conclude that Jesus killed her. Laurence Perrine, however, claims that "the question of Nancy's survival is the crowning uncertainty in a story whose consistent method is uncertainty" (307).

Characters and Themes

The two main characters of "That Evening Sun," Quentin and Nancy, each represent major themes of the story, initiation and racial division. Quentin's growing awareness of Nancy's situation initiates him into the mysteries of adulthood and violence. His childhood innocence gives way to knowledge of Nancy's pregnancy by Mr. Stovall, her despair and attempted suicide, and her terror of her husband. As a nine-year-old child, Quentin often seems not to understand fully what he observes, yet his adult self, looking back, shapes the story with mature insight that emerges indirectly. The strongest clue Faulkner provides that the child Quentin comes to realize the danger Jesus poses to Nancy is his final question, "Who will do our washing now, Father?" (309), implying that he expects her husband to murder her. In ironic contrast, his sister and brother merely bicker and call each other names throughout the story, oblivious to Nancy's peril.

Part of Quentin's initiation involves his dawning awareness of racial difference, but Faulkner's treatment of Nancy in the story goes beyond just Quentin's maturation to a critical analysis of race relations in the South. The first image of Nancy in the story is her strange dignity as she walks with a bundle of laundry on her head, topped with a black straw hat, down into the ditch near her house and crawls, with her head still high, through a fence. This ditch marks a boundary that the Compson children are forbidden to cross, a symbol of racial division. Later in the first section, after Quentin has told about Nancy's involvement with Mr. Stovall and her pregnancy, Nancy says to Quentin, "I aint nothing but a nigger. . . . It aint none of my fault" (293), a statement that raises the question of whether Nancy as a poor black woman in Jefferson at that time could have resisted Mr. Stovall's advances. After all, he kicks out her teeth in public with impunity.

Nancy may be powerless in the story to protect herself physically from Mr. Stovall or her husband, yet she defies each of them verbally. She chastises Mr. Stovall for not paying her, and she taunts Jesus that her "watermelon" "never come off of your vine" (292). (Emphasizing in turn his powerlessness as a black man, Jesus responds, "White man can come in my house, but I cant stop him.") In these ways, Nancy disrupts the abjectness of her status as a poor black woman. The story's ironic and critical treatment of race is further emphasized in the second section. Nancy, afraid to go to her home, is sleeping on a pallet in the Compson children's room, and says again, "I aint nothing but a nigger," prompting five-year-old Jason to say later "I aint a nigger" (298). These repetitions of the racist term call attention to the racial divide in society, while simultaneously interrogating the assumptions behind it through the irony of Jason's childishness and Nancy's bitter rebelliousness. Laurence Perrine concludes that the story "is about fear and the gulf separating the white and black communities which is both cause and result of that fear" (307).

"TURNABOUT" (1932)

Representative of Faulkner's stories about war is "Turnabout," first published in 1932 in *The Saturday Evening Post* (with the title spelled "Turn

About") and later in *Dr. Martino and Other Stories* (1934) and *Collected Stories* (1950). Typical of the genre, "Turnabout" pays tribute to the reckless courage of English and American soldiers in World War I, but the story deepens the formula by also indicting the senseless loss of life in wartime. In *The Collected Stories*, "Turnabout" is grouped with other stories of World War I in "The Wasteland" section of *The Collected Stories*, such as "Ad Astra" and "All the Dead Pilots" (in which the Sartoris twins appear), "Victory," and "Crevasse."

Characters and Structure

The central characters in "Turnabout" are a mature American fighter pilot, Captain Bogard, and a teen-aged English midshipman named Claude Hope. An omniscient third-person narrator tells the story from Bogard's point of view. In the first episode, Bogard meets young Hope passed out on a street in a French port late in the war. Bogard's fellow Americans mock Hope's callow foppishness, assuming he has never faced combat, and Bogard invites him to come along on a bombing raid. The story is symmetrically shaped around two ironically contrasted bombing missions, one in the air and one on water, in both of which bombs malfunction. In the first, Hope realizes that an unfired bomb is dangling from the wing of the airplane and tries to warn the American crew. When they ignore him, he assumes they know what they are doing and marvels at their bravery in landing the plane while dragging the bomb. In the turnabout of the title, Hope invites Bogard to join him and his fellow midshipman Ronnie Boyce Smith on a mission on their small torpedo boat. The danger they face in trying to launch a torpedo that initially fails to disengage convinces Bogard of their bravery.

Themes

Faulkner's rendering of the two bombing raids is skillfully suspenseful, creating a vivid sense of heroic coolness in battle that glamorizes combat, consistent with slick, commercial stories about war. The ending of the story, though, challenges this romantic view of war. In two short bulletins, the reader learns that Hope and Boyce Smith are missing in action, and Bogard has been commended for a foolhardy but successful mission to bomb the enemy's headquarters. With a bravado evocative of the torpedo boaters, Bogard flew in close to the target before dropping his last two bombs, thinking "God! God! If they were all there—all the generals, the admirals, the presidents and the kings—theirs, ours—all of them" (*Collected Stories* 509). Ending the story in this way, as with the ending of *The Unvanquished*,

Faulkner questions the romance of violence. The earlier glorification of heroism turns to a bitter denunciation of the powers that waste lives.

"Turnabout" became the first of Faulkner's works to be filmed when Howard Hawks directed Faulkner's own screenplay in 1933 under the title *Today We Live* (Kawin, *Faulkner's MGM Screenplays*). The film version includes the major elements of "Turnabout," with the addition of a love triangle that provided a role for Joan Crawford as Ronnie's sister Ann. The love story further emphasized the theme of the devastating effect of World War I on the Lost Generation.

"BARN BURNING" (1939)

"Barn Burning" was first published in June 1939 in *Harper's Magazine*, and it won the first O. Henry Memorial Award for best short story. Faulkner planned to make "Barn Burning" part of *The Hamlet* in the early stages of writing that novel, but he eventually decided it had no place in it. A much revised and shortened version of it appears in *The Hamlet*, but it is filtered through V. K. Ratliff's point of view, turning tragedy into comedy, according to Millgate (*Achievement* 66–67), "a tall tale lacking Sarty's agony" (Diane Brown Jones, *A Reader's Guide to the Short Stories of William Faulkner* 8). In "Barn Burning," 10-year-old Sarty Snopes defies his father Ab Snopes by revealing his father's plans to burn down the barn of Major de Spain, the aristocratic landlord for whom Snopes is a sharecropper in Yoknapatawpha County.

The story begins with a rural trial in another county in which Sarty is nearly required to give evidence against his father in a case involving a previous barn burning. Sarty (short for Colonel Sartoris) knows he is expected to lie for his father, who clearly has burned down Mr. Harris's barn. However, Harris backs off from putting Sarty in the position of testifying against his father, and Ab Snopes is acquitted from lack of evidence but ordered to leave the county. Over the course of the story, Sarty begins to question blood loyalty at the cost of justice, leading to his desperate decision ultimately to expose his father as a barn burner. At the end of the story, Sarty believes his father has been killed, and he knows he cannot return to his family.

Ab Snopes comes into conflict with Major de Spain when he tracks manure on an expensive French rug in de Spain's mansion, a symbol to young Sarty of order and dignity: "*Hit's big as a courthouse* he thought quietly, with a surge of peace and joy whose reason he could not have thought into words, being too young for that" (*Collected Stories* 10). Ordered by de Spain to clean the rug, Snopes damages it permanently. When de Spain imposes a fine of 20 bushels of corn for the cost of the rug, Snopes ulti-mately retaliates by burning his barn.

Interpretations of the story vary. Often critics read it in psychological terms as a rite of passage narrative, focusing on Sarty's initiation from blind loyalty to family into a sense of ethical individualism (Franklin; Volpe, *Reader's Guide to Short Stories*). Conversely, Jane Hiles interprets Sarty as repeating his father's tendency toward aggression and flight (Hiles). Other critics focus on the social and economic contexts that shape the conflict between Ab Snopes and Major de Spain (Zender, "Character and Sym-bol"). Although some critics identify Ab Snopes with the devil (Volpe, *Reader's Guide to Short Stories* 236), others see him as a victim of an op-pressive class system. The rich complexity of the story has earned it a place in the highest rank of American short stories.

"TOMORROW" (1940, 1949)

"Tomorrow" was published in *The Saturday Evening Post* in Novem-ber 1940 and in *Knight's Gambit* (1949), a collection of stories loosely connected by the character of Gavin Stevens, a lawyer who acts as a detective to solve the mysteries at the heart of the stories. "Tomorrow," like the novel *Light in August*, takes the form of a crime or detective story in which who committed the crime is not in question. Rather, in the case of "Tomorrow," the focus is on why a trial to acquit a man who killed in self-defense resulted in a hung jury. The dissenting juror's motive is the mystery at the heart of the story. The juror, Jackson Fentry, is the central character of the story, but the story's discourse keeps him at a distance, revealing his story indirectly through the filter of several oral storytellers.

The primary narrator is Charles "Chick" Mallison, looking back to a time 20 years earlier when his uncle Gavin Stevens was the defense at-torney in a murder trial. A man named Bookwright in self-defense killed Buck Thorpe, a ne'er-do-well who was running off with Bookwright's daughter. Stevens lost the self-defense case because one man, Stonewall Jackson Fentry, refused to vote for conviction, resulting in a hung jury. Twelve-year-old Chick accompanied his uncle to a remote area 30 miles from Frenchman's Bend to learn more about Fentry.

Chick reports the accounts of people who knew Fentry; they tell how, about 20 years before, Fentry had gone to Frenchman's Bend to work in a sawmill. One day a sick woman in the last stages of preg-nancy, abandoned by her husband, collapsed at the sawmill. Fentry, a poor uneducated man, took her in and cared for her, eventually asking her to marry him. As the birth of her baby approached, sensing she would not live, she agreed to the marriage, despite already having a husband. Shortly after a baby boy was born, a preacher married the couple, but she died soon after. Fentry devotedly raised the child for three years before the woman's brothers came to take him. They claimed that, since their sister had still been married to her first husband, Fentry had no legal right to the child. Fentry's devotion to the boy, who grew up to become Buck Thorpe, prevented him from voting to convict Thorpe's killer. Stevens, now understanding, said to his nephew, "The lowly and invincible of the earth—to endure and endure and then endure, tomorrow and tomorrow and tomorrow. Of course he wasn't going to vote Bookwright free" (Faulkner qtd. in Yellin and Connors).

"Tomorrow" is one of the most effective stories in *Knight's Gambit*. It transcends the detective story formula through the artful portrayal of Fentry; he is presented through the various layers of oral narration as a humble man with the capacity to love selflessly and to endure hardship. As Edmond Volpe notes, Fentry is an example of characters in Faulkner's fiction with the quality of figures from legend; they live close to the natural world (such as the convict in *Old Man* and Sam Fathers in *The Bear*) and take strength from the harshness and simplicity of their circumstances. Volpe identifies "Tomorrow" as an expression of Faulkner's "faith in man, in his capacity to love, his strength to endure anguish and hardship" (*A Reader's Guide to William Faulkner: The Short Stories* 243).

Horton Foote adapted "Tomorrow" as a television play in 1960 and again as a feature film starring Robert Duvall in 1972. Foote's sensitive adaptation, Duvall's finely etched performance, and the austere black-and-white photography of Alan Green combine to make the film the finest media adaptation of Faulkner's work to date.

THREE FAMOUS SHORT NOVELS (1958)

Spotted Horses (1931, 1940)

Faulkner's flair for comedy is evident in "Spotted Horses," a story first published in *Scribner's Magazine* in June 1931 and later anthologized in *Uncollected Stories of William Faulkner*, subsequently expanded as part of *The Hamlet* (1940), and revised slightly for inclusion in *The Portable Faulkner*. The longer version included in *Three Famous Short Novels* is from *The Hamlet*.

The core action in *Spotted Horses* is the duplicitous sale of some wild ponies to unsuspecting farmers in Frenchman's Bend (a poor settlement southeast of Jefferson in Yoknapatawpha County). When the buyers prove unable to catch the horses, the animals run wild through the settlement. This summary, though, does no justice to the rich colorfulness of the narrative, which is told by an omniscient narrator with much of the flavor of an oral storyteller filtered through Faulkner's poetic prose style. Early versions of the story employed explicitly oral narrative, and the published versions retain vestiges of it. Malcolm Cowley wrote that it would not be too much to call *Spotted Horses* "the funniest American story since Mark Twain" (*Portable Faulkner* 366).

The story begins when Flem Snopes and a Texan named Buck Hipps arrive in Frenchman's Bend with a group of wild horses tied together with wire. The men lounging at Jody Varner's store cannot resist bidding on the horses, despite the mockery of the traveling sewing machine salesman V. K. Ratliff, who guesses that Snopes is not to be trusted. One of the men who foolishly buys a horse is Henry Armstid (who also appears in *As I Lay Dying* and *Light in August*). He gives his wife's hard-earned money to Flem Snopes for a horse, even though the Texan refuses to sell him one and tells Mrs. Armstid to get the money back from Snopes. When the horses get loose, one tramples Armstid, breaking his legs. Later, after the Texan has left town, Mrs. Armstid tries to sue Snopes for her money but she loses the suit because Snopes claims the horses belonged to the Texan, who took the money with him. The long-suffering dignity of Mrs. Armstid adds a note of poignancy to the story.

Another dupe of the horse-selling scam is Flem's cousin, Eck Snopes, a blacksmith with a young son named Wallstreet Panic Snopes. Eck, one of the few decent and honest members of the Snopes clan, gets a free horse for buying the first one of the group. However, the bonus horse runs through Mrs. Littlejohn's boarding house on a hilarious rampage before injuring Vernon Tull (the neighbor who helps the Bundrens in *As I Lay Dying*). Mrs. Tull sues Eck Snopes for damages, but her suit also fails because there was no bill of sale.

The gaudy, untamable horses in the story are described in heightened language that endows them with a fascinating desirability. Flem Snopes literally capitalizes on their allure; he is an unscrupulous entrepreneur who uses the money from his horse-trading deals to launch himself, over the course of the Snopes trilogy, from the poky *Hamlet* of Frenchman's Bend to *The Town* of Jefferson where he becomes president of a bank and acquires the de Spain *Mansion*. The comedy of *Spotted Horses* thus serves the satirical purpose of demonstrating the rise of "Snopesism," a money-grubbing invasive force personified by Flem Snopes that encroaches upon the innocence and traditionalism of Yoknapatawpha County.

Old Man (1939, 1946)

Old Man was first published as part of *The Wild Palms* (1939) in counterpoint with the work of that title and then reprinted separately in *The Portable Faulkner* in 1946. Later, the original title of the contrapuntal novel, *If I Forget Thee, Jerusalem*, was restored. Although Faulkner allowed *Old Man* to be published separately, he claimed that the two narratives formed an integral whole, and there are significant thematic and structural parallels and ironic oppositions linking the parts. Both stories focus on a man and a pregnant woman in transit, but the outcomes of the pregnancies and the relationships are starkly contrasting.

Old Man is set during the historic Mississippi River flood of 1927. The main character, identified only as the Tall Convict, is a young man serving a 15-year sentence for attempted train robbery at the Mississippi state prison at Parchman. When a levee breaks nearby, he is turned loose in a small rowboat and sent to bring back a woman trapped in a tree and a man on a cottonhouse. Swept away by the current, the convict is presumed drowned, but he finds the woman in the tree and intends to complete his mission and return to prison. However, unable to resist the raging river (the Old Man of the title), the pair drift along until the woman goes into labor. The tall convict manages to deliver her baby on a snake-infested Indian mound, and they continue down the river. For 10 days, they stay with an alligator-hunter in a peaceful interlude but when a levee is blown up for flood control, they find themselves back on the river. Eventually, the Tall Convict returns the woman with her baby along with the skiff to his starting place. Accused of trying to escape, he has 10 more years added to his sentence.

On its surface, *Old Man* functions as an adventure story of man against nature, and the scenes in which the convict struggles against the overwhelming force of the river are powerfully rendered. Peter Lurie identifies how early readings of *The Wild Palms* interpreted the meaning of the flood as "an emblem for an omnipotent fate or for the continuous flow of time" (*Vision's Immanence* 213 note 5). However, Faulkner also embeds in the story a subtle critique of popular fiction that subverts the conventions of commercial adventure and romance stories.

Faulkner thought of *Old Man* as comic. He told students at the University of Virginia that he burdened the convict with a pregnant woman because it "made it funnier. To me all this is funny" (Gwynn and Blotner 176). Faulkner's sense of humor is bleakly sardonic. He has the convict land in jail in the first place because he took dime novels seriously and modeled his holdup of a train on ones in the *Detectives' Gazette* (*Three*

Famous Short Novels 79). Rather than falling in love with the pregnant woman he rescues, the convict thinks when he meets her: "*This, out of all the female meat that walks, is what I have to be caught in a runaway boat with*" (106). Later, the momentary thought of sex with her fills him with "a kind of savage and horrified revulsion" (180). The greatest irony of the novel is that, after finding freedom on the river, all the convict aspires to do is return to prison.

Despite the story's implicit critique of the conventions of popular fiction, a 1997 Hallmark Hall of Fame television adaptation appropriated the prestige of Faulkner's authorship to present a slickly commercialized version. "Playing up the story's sentimental potential—and dramatically altering its ending, turning the convict into a romantic hero who at the end of the story goes free and falls in love—the film reveals the way the culture industry can find sentimental material where it wants to and when doing so serves commercial ends" (Lurie, *Vision's Immanence* 213 note 7).

The Bear (1942)

Faulkner started writing *The Bear* as a section of *Go Down, Moses*, a work he thought of as a novel composed of interrelated stories. However, needing money, he got $1,000 from *The Saturday Evening Post* for a separate version of the story published in May of 1942. Then he went on to write a major section that made the overall story significantly deeper and more profound. The version published in *Three Famous Short Novels* in 1958 was the longer version that appeared in *Go Down, Moses*. This version of *The Bear* is a complex work that weaves together two major strands in the life of young Isaac (Ike) McCaslin, born in 1867: his initiation into manhood through hunting rituals in the period from 1877–85, and his repudiation in 1888 of his inheritance because of guilt associated with slavery in previous generations.

The Bear consists of five sections. The first three narrate the stages in Ike's initiation as a hunter from ages 10 to 16 under the guidance of Sam Fathers, a son of the Chickasaw chief Ikkemotubbe and a quadroon slave. Over six years, Fathers tutors Ike in the art of hunting, instilling in him a deep respect for nature. Each year, hunting parties track a bear called Old Ben, who takes on a mythic stature as a symbol of the wilderness. At the end of the story's first section, only after putting away his gun, compass, and watch, Ike earns his first glimpse of Old Ben.

In the second section, Ike is 13 and has killed his first deer the year before, a rite of passage that Fathers marked by smearing blood on Ike's face. The hunting party traps a wild mongrel dog, a "fyce," that Fathers names

Lion and keeps to track Ben. Boon Hogganbeck, the camp's rough handyman who, like Sam Fathers, is also part Chickasaw, befriends the dog and lets it sleep with him. Ike thinks "That was the way it should have been. Sam was the chief, the prince; Boon, the plebeian, was his huntsman. Boon should have nursed the dogs" (*Three Famous Short Novels* 214–15). At the end of the second section, General Compson, a member of the hunting party, shoots Old Ben, but he only draws blood without killing the bear.

The following year, narrated in the third section, the hunt for Old Ben reaches a climax. When Lion is fatally wounded by the bear, Boon jumps on Old Ben's back and stabs him in the heart. "For an instant they almost resembled a piece of statuary: the clinging dog, the bear, the man astride its back, working and probing the buried blade" (*Three Famous Short Novels* 232). As Old Ben dies, Sam Fathers also collapses, as if his will to live vanishes with the wilderness that the bear symbolizes. Following Fathers's orders, Boon helps the old man die, his body ceremonially placed on a platform of saplings.

The fourth section abruptly shifts from a focus on hunting to Ike's extended consideration (rendered in a streaming, stylized prose) of his family's history. Now 21 in 1888, Ike discusses with his cousin McCaslin (Cass) Edmonds their mutual inheritance and studies the plantation commissary ledgers kept by Ike's grandfather, Lucius Quintus Carothers McCaslin, and his twin sons, Ike's father Theophilus (Buck) and his brother Amodeus (Buddy) McCaslin. The ledgers contain cryptic entries that Ike interprets as evidence that his grandfather had a mulatto daughter named Tomasina (Tomey) in 1810 by his slave Eunice, and that he then committed incest with Tomey and as a result Eunice drowned herself on Christmas Day of 1832. Tomey died giving birth to a son, Tomey's Turl. This knowledge convinces Ike that his inherited land—and the whole South—is cursed. He tries to assuage his family's guilt by paying restitution to several descendants of Tomey's Turl, but he meets with limited success. Finally, he repudiates his inheritance, leaving it in the hands of his cousin Cass.

The final section of the story moves back in time a few years, to 1885, two years after the deaths of Old Ben, Lion, and Sam Fathers. Ike returns one more time to their graves in the Big Woods, where nearby a lumber company is now cutting down the forest. He finds Boon insanely beating the broken pieces of his gun together while squirrels scamper overhead, a reminder of the wilderness that is vanishing with the encroachment of industrialization.

In both narrative strands of *The Bear*, Ike McCaslin is searching, first in the woods and then in the ledgers, for an understanding of his relationship to the natural and social worlds. Sam Fathers is his spiritual mentor who teaches him humility and responsibility in relation to nature, just as his cousin Cass Edmonds tries to teach him his responsibility to his familial inheritance. Ike, though, renounces his responsibility to his family's curse, arguing to his cousin that the land was never theirs to own, just as (by implication) other human beings were never theirs to own (*Three Famous Short Novels* 246–49). Challenged by Cass, Ike rationalizes further that the answers to the burden of the past, as Arthur Kinney summarizes, "lie not with him or with Cass but with the blacks. Their endurance alone will save both blacks and whites. . . . [but] Cass can no more tolerate Ike's excessive patronizing of blacks than he can tolerate Ike's own self-patronizing" (Kinney, *Go Down, Moses* 88). Faulkner creates a dialectical discourse between the cousins that leaves unresolved any ultimate answers. Ike, though aspiring to be Christlike, ultimately turns away from life and is thus an unreliable moral center in *The Bear*.

ALTERNATIVE READING: POPULAR CULTURE CRITICISM

Critics of popular culture read literary texts as forms of entertainment distributed to broad audiences through mass media such as film, television, and popular print media. They examine the ways that literature as an artifact of popular culture reflects and shapes the values and experiences of mass audiences. The correlation of so-called highbrow art forms with elite social classes and so-called lowbrow forms with middle and lower social classes has become increasingly blurred in modern and postmodern culture. The work of William Faulkner provides a particularly rich source of insight into the blurring of highbrow and lowbrow cultural categories and the impact of the marketplace on how he wrote. On the one hand, Faulkner saw himself as a "sincere" artist "of the first class" who should be free of "economic responsibilities" (Blotner, *Selected Letters* 122), yet he felt compelled to produce popular fiction and screenplays that he called trash and junk and that he blamed for corrupting his artistic writing. On the other hand, Faulkner's work in popular genres provided him with material that he used in creating his "serious" work.

Obvious examples among his short fiction include his incorporation of sentimental *Saturday Evening Post* elements into a work such as *The Bear* and his use of the Tall Convict's obsession with dime novels as a key element in *Old Man*. Faulkner was capable of balancing the commercial demands of the marketplace with his own standards of art. In *The Bear* Faulkner was able to use one strand of his narrative to appeal to a mass audience who would read the deaths of Old Ben, Lion, and Sam Fathers as a tear-jerkingly satisfying resolution of Ike's adventures in the Big Woods; at the same time, he was such a great craftsman that he was able to juxtapose that material with the ledgers section of the short novel version of the story to create a magnificently complex exploration of Ike's relationship to the social, historical, and natural worlds and its moral implications. In *Old Man*, Faulkner managed to satisfy both the demands of a tale of adventure and natural disaster and a darkly humorous satire of the conventions of such popular formula fiction.

Faulkner also managed—to a lesser degree—to contain and channel what he feared was the corrupting influence of Hollywood so that his work there maintained a modicum of integrity to his larger goals as an artist. His work adapting his story "Turnabout" for the film *Today We Live* provides additional dimension to the story that links it to such major fiction as *The Sound and the Fury*, as Bruce Kawin has demonstrated in his *Faulkner and Film* and his edition of Faulkner's MGM screenplays. Taking a cue from Faulkner, critics have long dismissed as minor or flawed such works as *The Unvanquished*, *Pylon*, and *If I Forget Thee, Jerusalem*. Seen through the lens of popular culture criticism, however, these works provide insight into Faulkner's ability to critique popular media while writing within that very media.

The tension between highbrow and lowbrow cultural forms, between art and commerce, inspired Faulkner to bridge the perceived gap in these categories and to synthesize them. This tension that frustrated Faulkner also served to fuel his creative energies. As with his ambivalent treatment of the myth of the old South and his balancing of oral tradition and modernist experimentation in his fiction, Faulkner proved himself capable of juxtaposing disparate (even commercial) elements into great, enduring works of art that explored the human heart in conflict with itself.

Selected Bibliography

Parenthetical references to Faulkner's novels in the text are to the Vintage International editions.

WORKS BY WILLIAM FAULKNER

The Marble Faun. Boston: Four Seas, 1924.

Soldiers' Pay. New York: Boni and Liveright, 1926.

Mosquitoes. New York: Boni and Liveright, 1927.

Sartoris. New York: Harcourt, Brace, 1929.

The Sound and the Fury. New York: Jonathan Cape and Harrison Smith, 1929; Corrected Text, Vintage, 1990.

As I Lay Dying. New York: Jonathan Cape and Harrison Smith, 1930; Corrected Text, Vintage, 1991.

Sanctuary. New York: Jonathan Cape and Harrison Smith, 1931.

These 13. New York: Jonathan Cape and Harrison Smith, 1931.

Light in August. New York: Harrison Smith and Robert Haas, 1932; Corrected Text, Vintage, 1990.

Doctor Martino and Other Stories. New York: Harrison Smith and Robert Haas, 1934.

Pylon. New York: Harrison Smith and Robert Haas, 1935.

Absalom, Absalom! New York: Random House, 1936; Corrected Text, Vintage, 1990.

The Unvanquished. New York: Random House, 1938; Corrected Text, Vintage, 1991.

The Wild Palms. New York: Random House, 1939.

The Hamlet. New York: Random House, 1940.

Go Down, Moses. New York: Random House, 1942.

Intruder in the Dust. New York: Random House, 1948.

Knight's Gambit. New York: Random House, 1949.

Collected Stories. New York: Random House, 1950.

Requiem for a Nun. New York: Random House, 1951.

A Fable. New York: Random House, 1954.

The Town. New York: Random House, 1957.

The Mansion. New York: Random House, 1959.

Three Famous Short Novels: Spotted Horses, Old Man, and The Bear. New York: Random House, 1961.

The Reivers. New York: Random House, 1962.

POSTHUMOUS PUBLICATIONS

Essays, Speeches and Public Letters by William Faulkner. Ed. James B. Meriwether. New York: Random House, 1966.

New Orleans Sketches. Ed. Carvel Collins. New York: Random House, 1968.

Flags in the Dust. Ed. Douglas Day. New York: Random House, 1973.

The Marionettes: A Play in One Act. Ed. Noel Polk. [Charlottesville]: Bibliographical Society of the University of Virginia and the University Press of Virginia, 1975.

Uncollected Stories. Ed. Joseph L. Blotner. New York: Random House, 1979.

BIOGRAPHIES, LETTERS, AND INTERVIEWS

Blotner, Joseph. *Faulkner: A Biography*. 2 vols. New York: Random House, 1974. One-vol. rev. ed., 1984. (Parenthetical references in the text are to the one-vol. ed.)

———. "Faulkner in Hollywood." *Man and the Movies*. Ed. W. R. Robinson with assistance from George Garrett. Baton Rouge: Louisiana State UP, 1967. 261–303.

———, ed. *Selected Letters of William Faulkner*. New York: Vintage, 1978.

Cowley, Malcolm. *The Faulkner-Cowley File: Letters and Memories, 1944–1962*. New York: Viking, 1966.

———, ed. *The Portable Faulkner*. New York: Viking, 1946.

Dardis, Tom. *Some Time in the Sun*. New York: Limelight, 1988.

Doyle, Don H. *Faulkner's County: The Historical Roots of Yoknapatawpha*. Chapel Hill: U of North Carolina P, 2001.

Fant, Joseph L., and Robert Ashley, eds. *Faulkner at West Point*. New York: Random House, 1964.

Gray, Richard. *The Life of William Faulkner*. Cambridge, MA: Blackwell, 1994.

Gwynn, Frederick L., and Joseph L. Blotner, eds. *Faulkner in the University*. Charlottesville: UP of Virginia, 1995.

Inge, M. Thomas, ed. *Conversations with William Faulkner*. Jackson: UP of Mississippi, 1999.

Meriwether, James B., and Michael Millgate, eds. *Lion in the Garden: Interviews with William Faulkner, 1926–1962*. New York: Random House, 1968.

Minter, David. *William Faulkner: His Life and Works*. Baltimore, MD: Johns Hopkins UP, 1980.

Oates, Stephen B. *William Faulkner: The Man and the Artist*. New York: Harper and Row, 1987.

Parini, Jay. *One Matchless Time: A Life of William Faulkner*. New York: HarperCollins, 2004.

Snell, Susan. *Phil Stone of Oxford: A Vicarious Life*. Athens: U of Georgia P, 1991.

Wasson, Ben. *Count No 'Count: Flashbacks to Faulkner*. Jackson: UP of Mississippi, 1983.

Watson, James G., ed. *Thinking of Home: William Faulkner's Letters to His Mother and Father, 1918–1925*. New York: Norton, 1992.

———. *William Faulkner: Self-Presentation and Performance*. Austin: U of Texas P, 2000.

Wilde, Meta Carpenter, and Orin Borsten. *A Loving Gentleman: The Love Story of William Faulkner and Meta Carpenter*. New York: Simon and Schuster, 1976.

Williamson, Joel. *William Faulkner and Southern History*. New York: Oxford UP, 1993.

CONTEMPORARY REVIEWS OF FAULKNER'S WORK

Inge, M. Thomas. *William Faulkner: The Contemporary Reviews*. New York: Cambridge UP, 1995.

CRITICAL STUDIES OF FAULKNER'S WORK

Atkinson, Ted. *Faulkner and the Great Depression: Aesthetics, Ideology, and Cultural Politics*. Athens: U of Georgia P, 2006.

Bauer, Margaret Donovan. *William Faulkner's Legacy: "What Shadow, What Stain, What Mark."* Gainesville: UP of Florida, 2005.

Bleikasten, André. "Faulkner From a European Perspective." *The Cambridge Companion to William Faulkner*. Ed. Philip M. Weinstein. Cambridge: Cambridge UP, 1995. 75–95.

———. *The Ink of Melancholy: Faulkner's Novels from "The Sound and the Fury" to "Light in August"*. Bloomington: Indiana UP, 1990.

Bloom, Harold, ed. *Modern Critical Views: William Faulkner*. New York: Chelsea House, 1986.

Brooks, Cleanth. *On the Prejudices, Predilections, and Firm Beliefs of William Faulkner: Essays*. Baton Rouge: Louisiana State UP, 1987.

———.*William Faulkner: First Encounters*. New Haven, CT: Yale UP, 1983.

———. *William Faulkner: Toward Yoknapatawpha and Beyond*. New Haven, CT: Yale UP, 1978.

———. *William Faulkner: The Yoknapatawpha Country*. Baton Rouge: Louisiana State UP, 1990.

Broughton, Panthea Reid. "Faulkner's Cubist Novels." *"A Cosmos of My Own": Faulkner and Yoknapatawpha, 1980*. Ed. Doreen Fowler and Ann J. Abadie. Jackson: UP of Mississippi, 1981. 59–94.

Budd, Louis. "Playing Hide and Seek with William Faulkner: The Publicly Private Artist." *Faulkner and Popular Culture: Faulkner and Yoknapatawpha 1988*. Ed. Doreen Fowler and Ann J. Abadie. Jackson: UP of Mississippi, 1990. 34–58.

Carothers, James B. *William Faulkner's Short Stories*. Ann Arbor: U of Michigan Research P, 1985.

Clarke, Deborah. *Robbing the Mother: Women in Faulkner*. Jackson: UP of Mississippi, 1994.

Coughlan, Robert. *The Private World of William Faulkner*. New York: Harper, 1954.

Davis, Thadious M. *Faulkner's "Negro": Art and the Southern Context*. Baton Rouge: Louisiana State UP, 1983.

———. "From Jazz Syncopation to Blues Elegy: Faulkner's Development of Black Characterization." *Faulkner and Race: Faulkner and Yoknapatawpha 1986*. Ed. Doreen Fowler and Ann J. Abadie. Jackson: UP of Mississippi, 1987. 70–92.

Duvall, John N. "Faulkner's Crying Game: Male Homosexual Panic." *Faulkner and Gender: Faulkner and Yoknapatawpha, 1994*. Ed. Donald M. Kartiganer and Ann J. Abadie. Jackson: UP of Mississippi, 1986. 41–57.

———. *Faulkner's Marginal Couple: Invisible, Outlaw, and Unspeakable Communities*. Austin: U of Texas P, 1990.

———. "Toni Morrison and the Anxiety of Faulknerian Influence." *Unflinching Gaze: Morrison and Faulkner Re-Envisioned*. Ed. Carol A. Kolmerten, Stephen M. Ross, and Judith Bryant Wittenberg. Jackson: UP of Mississippi, 1997. 3–16.

Fargnoli, A. Nicholas, and Michael Golay. *William Faulkner A to Z: The Essential Reference to His Life and Work*. New York: Checkmark Books, 2002.

Ferguson, James. *Faulkner's Short Fiction*. Knoxville: U of Tennessee P, 1991.

Fowler, Doreen. *Faulkner: The Return of the Repressed*. Charlottesville: UP of Virginia, 1997.

Frisch, Mark. "Latin America." *A William Faulkner Encyclopedia*. Ed. Robert W. Hamblin and Charles A. Peek. Westport, CT: Greenwood P, 1999. 219–22.

Grimwood, Michael. *Heart in Conflict: Faulkner's Struggles with Vocation*. Athens: U of Georgia P, 1987.

Guerard, Albert. J. *The Triumph of the Novel: Dickens, Dostoevsky, Faulkner.* Chicago: U of Chicago P, 1976.

Hamblin, Robert W., and Charles A. Peek, eds. *A William Faulkner Encyclopedia.* Westport, CT: Greenwood, 1999.

Hoffman, Frederick J. *William Faulkner.* 2nd ed. rev. New York: Twayne, 1966.

———, and Olga W. Vickery, eds. *William Faulkner: Three Decades of Criticism.* East Lansing: Michigan State UP, 1960.

———, and Olga W. Vickery, eds. *William Faulkner: Two Decades of Criticism.* East Lansing: Michigan State College P, 1951.

Howe, Irving. *William Faulkner: A Critical Study.* 4th ed. Chicago, IL: Ivan R. Dee, 1991.

Inge, M. Thomas. *William Faulkner.* New York: Overlook Duckworth, 2006.

Irwin, John T. *Doubling and Incest/Repetition and Revenge: A Speculative Reading of Faulkner.* Exp. Ed. Baltimore, MD: Johns Hopkins UP, 1996.

Jehlen, Myra. *Class and Character in Faulkner's South.* New York: Columbia UP, 1976.

Jones, Anne Goodwyn. "'The Kotex Age': Women, Popular Culture, and *The Wild Palms.*" *Faulkner and Popular Culture: Faulkner and Yoknapatawpha 1988.* Ed. Doreen Fowler and Ann J. Abadie. Jackson: UP of Mississippi, 1990. 142–62.

———. "'Like a Virgin': Faulkner, Sexual Cultures, and the Romance of Resistance." *Faulkner in Cultural Context: Faulkner and Yoknapatawpha 1995.* Ed. Donald M. Kartiganer and Ann J. Abadie. Jackson: UP of Mississippi, 1997. 39–74.

Jones, Diane Brown. *A Reader's Guide to the Short Stories of William Faulkner.* New York: G. K. Hall, 1994.

Karl, Frederick R. *William Faulkner: American Writer.* New York: Weidenfeld and Nicolson, 1989.

Kartiganer, Donald. *The Fragile Thread: The Meaning of Form in Faulkner's Novels.* Amherst: U of Massachusetts P, 1979.

Kawin, Bruce F. *Faulkner and Film.* New York: Frederick Ungar, 1977.

———, ed. *Faulkner's MGM Screenplays.* Knoxville: U of Tennessee P, 1982.

———. "Sharecropping in the Golden Land." *Faulkner and Popular Culture: Faulkner and Yoknapatawpha 1988.* Ed. Doreen Fowler and Ann J. Abadie. Jackson: UP of Mississippi, 1990. 196–206.

Kinney, Arthur F. *Faulkner's Narrative Poetics: Style as Vision.* Amherst: U of Massachusetts P, 1978.

Kolmerten, Carol A., Stephen M. Ross, and Judith Bryant Wittenberg, eds. *Unflinching Gaze: Morrison and Faulkner Re-Envisioned.* Jackson: UP of Mississippi, 1997.

Kreiswirth, Martin. *William Faulkner: The Making of a Novelist.* Athens: U of Georgia P, 1983.

Labatt, Blair. *Faulkner the Storyteller.* Tuscaloosa: U of Alabama P, 2005.

Ladd, Barbara. *Nationalism and the Color Line in George W. Cable, Mark Twain, and William Faulkner.* Baton Rouge: Louisiana State UP, 1996.

LaLonde, Christopher A. *William Faulkner and the Rites of Passage.* Macon, GA: Mercer UP, 1996.

Leary, Lewis. *William Faulkner of Yoknapatawpha County.* New York: Crowell, 1973.

Lee, A. Robert, ed. *William Faulkner: The Yoknapatawpha Fiction.* New York: St. Martin's, 1990.

Lester, Cheryl. "To Market, To Market: *The Portable Faulkner.*" *Criticism* 29 (1987): 371–89.

Lurie, Peter. "Cultural-Studies Criticism." *A Companion to Faulkner Studies.* Ed. Charles A. Peek and Robert W. Hamblin Westport, CT: Greenwood P, 2004. 163–95.

———. *Vision's Immanence: Faulkner, Film, and the Popular Imagination.* Baltimore: Johns Hopkins UP, 2004.

Marius, Richard. *Reading Faulkner: Introductions to the First Thirteen Novels.* Comp. and ed. By Nancy Grisham Anderson. Knoxville: U of Tennessee P, 2006.

Matthews, John T. "Faulkner and Proletarian Literature." *Faulkner in Cultural Context: Faulkner and Yoknapatawpha 1995.* Ed. Donald M. Kartiganer and Ann J. Abadie. Jackson: UP of Mississippi, 1997. 166–90.

———. *The Play of Faulkner's Language.* Ithaca: Cornell UP, 1982.

Millgate, Michael. *The Achievement of William Faulkner.* Athens: U of Georgia P, 1989.

Minter, David. *Faulkner's Questioning Narratives: Fiction of His Major Phase, 1929–1932.* Urbana: U of Illinois P, 2004.

Moreland, Richard C. *Faulkner and Modernism: Rereading and Rewriting.* Madison: U of Wisconsin P, 1990.

Mortimer, Gail. *Faulkner's Rhetoric of Loss: A Study in Perception and Meaning.* Austin: U of Texas P, 1983.

Oakley, Helen. "William Faulkner and the Cold War: The Politics of Cultural Marketing." *Look Away! The U.S. South in New World Studies.* Ed. Jon Smith and Deborah Cohn. Durham, NC: Duke UP, 2004. 405–18.

Parker, Robert Dale. *Faulkner and the Novelistic Imagination.* Urbana: U of Illinois P, 1985.

———. "Sex and Gender, Feminine and Masculine: Faulkner and the Polymorphous Exchange of Cultural Binaries." *Faulkner and Gender: Faulkner and Yoknapatawpha 1994.* Ed. Donald M. Kartiganer and Ann J. Abadie. Jackson: UP of Mississippi, 1996. 73–96.

Pearce, Richard. *The Politics of Narration: James Joyce, William Faulkner, and Virginia Woolf.* New Brunswick, NJ: Rutgers UP, 1991.

Peek, Charles A., and Robert W. Hamblin, eds. *A Companion to Faulkner Studies.* Westport, CT: Greenwood, 2004.

Phillips, Gene D. *Fiction, Film, and Faulkner: The Art of Adaptation.* Knoxville: U of Tennessee P, 1988.

Polk, Noel. *Children of the Dark House: Text and Context in Faulkner*. Jackson: UP of Mississippi, 1998.

Putzel, Max. *Genius of Place: William Faulkner's Triumphant Beginnings*. Baton Rouge: Louisiana State UP, 1985.

Railey, Kevin. *Natural Aristocracy: History, Ideology, and the Production of William Faulkner*. Tuscaloosa: U of Alabama P, 1999.

Raschke, Debrah. "Modernist Criticism." *A Companion to Faulkner Studies*. Ed. Charles A. Peek and Robert W. Hamblin. Westport, CT: Greenwood P, 2004. 99–124.

Reed, Joseph W. *Faulkner's Narrative*. New Haven: Yale UP, 1973.

Roberts, Diane. *Faulkner and Southern Womanhood*. Athens: U of Georgia P, 1994.

Ross, Stephen M. *Fiction's Inexhaustible Voice: Speech and Writing in Faulkner*. Athens: U of Georgia P, 1989.

Ruppersburg, Hugh M. *Voice and Eye in Faulkner's Fiction*. Athens: U of Georgia P, 1983.

Schwartz, Lawrence H. *Creating Faulkner's Reputation: The Politics of Modern Literary Criticism*. Knoxville: U of Tennessee P, 1988.

Sensibar, Judith L. *The Origins of Faulkner's Art*. Austin: U of Texas P, 1984.

Singal, Daniel J. *William Faulkner: The Making of a Modernist*. Chapel Hill: U of North Carolina P, 1997.

Skei, Hans H. *Reading Faulkner's Best Short Stories*. Columbia: U of South Carolina P, 1999.

Slatoff, Walter J. *Quest for Failure: A Study of William Faulkner*. Ithaca, NY: Cornell UP, 1960.

Snead, James A. *Figures of Division: William Faulkner's Major Novels*. New York: Methuen, 1986.

Stavans, Ilan. "Beyond Translation: Jorge Luis Borges Revamps William Faulkner." *Look Away! The U.S. South in New World Studies*. Ed. Jon Smith and Deborah Cohn. Durham, NC: Duke UP, 2004. 495–504.

Sundquist, Eric J. *Faulkner: The House Divided*. Baltimore, MD: Johns Hopkins UP, 1983.

Swiggart, Peter. *The Art of Faulkner's Novels*. Austin: U of Texas P, 1962.

Swisher, Clarice, ed. *Readings on William Faulkner*. San Diego, CA: Greenhaven, 1998.

Towner, Theresa M. *Faulkner on the Color Line: The Later Novels*. Jackson: UP of Mississippi, 2000.

Tredell, Nicolas, ed. *William Faulkner:* The Sound and the Fury *and* As I Lay Dying. New York: Columbia UP, 1999.

Tuck, Dorothy. *Crowell's Handbook of Faulkner*. New York: Crowell, 1964.

Urgo, Joseph R. *Faulkner's Apocrypha: A Fable, Snopes, and the Spirit of Human Rebellion*. Jackson: UP of Mississippi, 1989.

Vickery, Olga. *The Novels of William Faulkner: A Critical Introduction*. Rev. ed. Baton Rouge: Louisiana State UP, 1995.

Volpe, Edmond L. *A Reader's Guide to William Faulkner: The Novels.* Syracuse, NY: Syracuse UP, 2003.

———. *A Reader's Guide to William Faulkner: The Short Stories.* Syracuse, NY: Syracuse UP, 2004.

Wadlington, Warwick. *Reading Faulknerian Tragedy.* Ithaca, NY: Cornell UP, 1987.

Wagner-Martin, Linda, ed. *William Faulkner: Four Decades of Criticism.* East Lansing: Michigan State UP, 1973.

———, ed. *William Faulkner: Six Decades of Criticism.* East Lansing: Michigan State UP, 2002.

Warren, Robert Penn, ed. *Faulkner: A Collection of Critical Essays.* Englewood Cliffs, NJ: Prentice-Hall, 1966.

Watson, James G. *William Faulkner: Letters and Fictions.* Austin: U of Texas P, 1987.

Weinstein, Philip M., ed. *The Cambridge Companion to William Faulkner.* New York: Cambridge UP, 1995.

———. *What Else But Love? The Ordeal of Race in Faulkner and Morrison.* New York: Columbia UP, 1996.

Welty, Eudora. *Eudora Welty On William Faulkner.* Jackson: UP of Mississippi, 2003.

Wittenberg, Judith B. *Faulkner: The Transfiguration of Biography.* Lincoln: U of Nebraska P, 1979.

Yamaguchi, Ryuichi. *Faulkner's Artistic Vision: The Bizarre and the Terrible.* Madison, NJ: Fairleigh Dickinson UP, 2004.

Zender, Karl F. *Faulkner and the Politics of Reading.* Baton Rouge: Louisiana State UP, 2002.

THE SOUND AND THE FURY (1929)

Contemporary Reviews

[Anonymous]. "Decayed Gentility." *The New York Times Book Review* November 10, 1929: 28.

Davenport, Basil. "Tragic Frustration." *Saturday Review of Literature* December 28, 1929: 601–02.

Fadiman, Clifton P. "Hardly Worth While." *The Nation* 130:3367 (January 15, 1930): 74–75.

Fitts, Dudley. "Two Aspects of Telemachus." *Hound and Horn* 3 (April-June 1930): 445–50.

Hansen, Harry. "The First Reader." [New York] *World* October 9, 1929: 16.

McClure, John [Julia K. W. Baker]. "Literature and Less: A Page on Books of the Day." [New Orleans] *Times-Picayune* June 29, 1930: 23.

Myers, Walter L. "Make-Beliefs." *Virginia Quarterly Review* 6 (January 1930): 139–48.

Saxon, Lyle. "A Family Breaks Up." *New York Herald Tribune Books* October 13, 1929: 3.

Smith, Henry Nash. "Three Southern Novels." *Southwest Review* 15 (1929): iii–iv.

Criticism

Aswell, Duncan. "The Recollection and the Blood: Jason's Role in *The Sound and the Fury.*" *Mississippi Quarterly* 21 (Summer 1968): 211–18.

Baum, Catherine B. "'The Beautiful One': Caddy Compson as Heroine of *The Sound and the Fury.*" *Modern Fiction Studies* 13 (Spring 1967): 33–44.

Benson, Jackson J. "Quentin Compson: Self-Portrait of a Young Artist's Emotions." *Twentieth Century Literature* 17 (July 1971): 143–59.

Blanchard, Margaret. "The Rhetoric of Communion: Voice in *The Sound and the Fury.*" *American Literature* 41 (January 1970): 555–65.

Bowling, Lawrence E. "Faulkner: The Theme of Pride in *The Sound and the Fury.*" *Modern Fiction Studies* 11 (Summer 1965): 129–39.

Brown, Arthur A. "Benjy, the Reader, and Death: At the Fence in *The Sound and the Fury.*" *Mississippi Quarterly* 48 (Summer 1995): 407–20.

Brown, May Cameron. "The Language of Chaos: Quentin Compson in *The Sound and the Fury.*" *American Literature* 51 (January 1980): 544–53.

Collins, Carvel. "The Interior Monologues of *The Sound and the Fury.*" *English Institute Essays 1952.* Ed. Alan S. Downer. New York: Columbia UP, 1954. 29–56.

Cowan, Michael H., ed. *Twentieth Century Interpretations of* The Sound and the Fury. Englewood Cliffs, NJ: Prentice-Hall, 1968.

Dickerson, Mary Jane. "'The Magician's Wand': Faulkner's Compson Appendix." *Mississippi Quarterly* 28 (Summer 1975): 317–37.

Duvall, John N. "Contextualizing *The Sound and the Fury:* Sex, Gender, and Community in Modern American Fiction." In Stephen Hahn and Arthur Kinney, eds. 101–07.

Faulkner, William. *The Sound and the Fury:* A Hypertext Edition. Ed. Stoicheff, Muri, Deshave, et al. Updated Mar. 2003. U of Saskatchewan. Accessed Jan. 9, 2006 <http://www.usask.ca/english/faulkner>

———. "An Introduction for *The Sound and the Fury*" (1972). In David Minter, ed. 225–28.

———. "An Introduction to *The Sound and the Fury*" (1973). In David Minter, ed. 228–32.

Feldstein, Richard. "Gerald Bland's Shadow." *Literature and Psychology* 31 (1981): 4–12.

Gresset, Michel. "Psychological Aspects of Evil in *The Sound and the Fury.*" *Mississippi Quarterly* 19 (Summer 1966): 143–53.

Hahn, Stephen, and Arthur F. Kinney. *Approaches to Teaching Faulkner's* The Sound and the Fury. New York: Modern Language Association, 1996.

Hornback, Vernon T., Jr. "The Uses of Time in Faulkner's *The Sound and the Fury*." *Papers on English Language and Literature* 1 (Winter 1965): 50–58.

Iser, Wolfgang. "Perception, Temporality, and Action as Modes of Subjectivity. William Faulkner: *The Sound and the Fury*." *The Implied Reader: Patterns of Communication in Prose Fiction from Bunyan to Beckett*. Baltimore: Johns Hopkins UP, 1974. 136–52.

Longley, John L. "'Who Never Had a Sister': A Reading of *The Sound and the Fury*." *Mosaic* 7 (Fall 1973): 35–53.

Lowrey, Perrin H. "Concepts of Time in *The Sound and the Fury*." *English Institute Essays 1952*. Ed. Alan S. Downer. New York: Columbia UP, 1954. 57–82.

Matthews, John T. *"The Sound and the Fury": Faulkner and the Lost Cause*. Boston: Twayne, 1991.

Mellard, James M. "Faulkner's Jason and the Tradition of Oral Narrative." *Journal of Popular Culture* 2 (Fall 1968): 195–210.

———. "*The Sound and the Fury*: Quentin Compson and Faulkner's 'Tragedy of Passion'." *Studies in the Novel* 2 (Spring 1970): 61–75.

———. "Type and Archetype: Jason Compson as 'Satirist'." *Genre* 4 (June 1971): 173–88.

Messerli, Douglas. "The Problem of Time in *The Sound and the Fury*: A Critical Reassessment and Reinterpretation." *The Southern Literary Journal* 6 (Spring 1974): 19–41.

Minter, David, ed. *The Sound and the Fury*. Norton Critical Edition. New York: Norton, 1994.

Polk, Noel, ed. *New Essays on* The Sound and the Fury. New York: Cambridge UP, 1993.

Ross, Stephen M. "Jason Compson and Sut Lovingood: Southwestern Humor as Stream of Consciousness." *Studies in the Novel* 8 (1976): 278–90.

——— and Noel Polk, eds. *Reading Faulkner: The Sound and the Fury*. Jackson: UP of Mississippi, 1996.

Trouard, Dawn. "Faulkner's Text Which Is Not One." In Noel Polk, ed. 23–69.

AS I LAY DYING (1930)

Contemporary Reviews

[Anonymous]. "A Witch's Brew." *The New York Times Book Review* October 19, 1930: 6.

Davenport, Basil. "In the Mire." *Saturday Review of Literature* November 22, 1930: 362.

Fadiman, Clifton P. "Morbidity in Fiction." *The Nation* 131: 3409 (November 5, 1930): 500–01.

McClure, John [Julia K. W. Baker]. "Literature and Less." [New Orleans] *Times-Picayune* October 26, 1930: 33.

Wade, John Donald. "The South in Its Fiction." *Virginia Quarterly Review* 7 (1931): 124–26.

White, Kenneth. "*As I Lay Dying* by William Faulkner." *New Republic* November 19, 1930: 27.

Criticism

Anderson, John D. "*As I Lay Dying*: Faulkner's Tour de Force One-Man Show." *Text and Performance Quarterly* (1996): 109–30.

Antonio, Mervin P. "Bringing *As I Lay Dying* to Life." Program Notes. *As I Lay Dying*. Adapted and directed by Frank Galati. Steppenwolf Theatre Company, June 28-August 13, 1995.

"'As I Lay Dying': Dance-drama based on Faulkner's novel, with choreographer-dancer Valerie Bettis." Creative Arts Television. <http://www.catarchive.com/detailPages/650509.html>

Bassett, John Earl. "*As I Lay Dying*: Family Conflict and Verbal Fiction." *The Journal of Narrative Technique* 11 (Spring 1981): 125–34.

Bedient, Calvin. "Pride and Nakedness: *As I Lay Dying*." *Modern Language Quarterly* 29 (March 1968): 61–76.

Blaine, Diana York. "The Abjection of Addie and Other Myths of the Maternal in *As I Lay Dying*." *Mississippi Quarterly* 47 (Summer 1994): 419–39.

Bleikasten, André. *Faulkner's* As I Lay Dying. Rev. and enlarged ed. Trans. Roger Little. Bloomington: U of Indiana P, 1973.

Branch, Watson. "Darl Bundren's 'Cubistic' Vision." *William Faulkner's* As I Lay Dying: A Critical Casebook. Ed. Dianne L. Cox. New York: Garland, 1985. 111–29.

Cox, Dianne L., ed. *William Faulkner's* As I Lay Dying: A Critical Casebook. New York: Garland, 1985.

Ferrer, Daniel. "*In omnis iam vocabuli mortem*: Representation of Absence of the Subject in William Faulkner's *As I Lay Dying*." *Oxford Literary Review* 5:1–2 (1982): 21–36.

Hale, Dorothy J. "*As I Lay Dying* 's Heterogeneous Discourse." *Novel* 23 (Fall 1989): 5–23.

Handy, William J. "*As I Lay Dying*: Faulkner's Inner Reporter." *Kenyon Review* 21 (Summer 1959): 437–51.

Hayes, Elizabeth. "Tension Between Darl and Jewel." *Southern Literary Journal* 24 (Spring 1992): 49–61.

Hemenway, Robert. "Enigmas of Being in *As I Lay Dying*." *Modern Fiction Studies* 16 (Summer 1970): 133–46.

Komar, Kathleen. "A Structural Study of *As I Lay Dying*." *Faulkner Studies I: An Annual of Research, Criticism, and Reviews*. Ed. Barnett Guttenberg, Miami: U of Miami P, 1980. 48–57.

Leath, Helen Lang. "'Will the Circle Be Unbroken?': An Analysis of Structure in *As I Lay Dying*." *Southwestern American Literature* 3 (1973): 61–68.

Logan, Elizabeth Ann. "A Study of Robert L. Flynn's *Journey to Jefferson*, an Adaptation of William Faulkner's *As I Lay Dying*." M. A. Thesis. Tulane U, 1967.

Luce, Dianne C. *As I Lay Dying/Annotated by Dianne C. Luce*. New York: Garland, 1990.

Palliser, Charles. "Fate and Madness: The Determinist Vision of Darl Bundren." *American Literature* 49 (January 1978): 619–33.

Rossky, William. "*As I Lay Dying*: The Insane World." *Texas Studies in Literature and Language* 4 (Spring 1962): 87–95.

Sadler, David F. "The Second Mrs. Bundren: Another Look at the Ending of *As I Lay Dying*." *American Literature* 37 (March 1965): 65–69.

Samway, Patrick, S. J. "Addie's Continued Presence in *As I Lay Dying*." *Southern Literature and Literary Theory*. Ed. Jefferson Humphries. Athens: U of Georgia P, 1990. 284–99.

Slaughter, Carolyn Norman. "*As I Lay Dying*: Demise of Vision." *American Literature* 61 (March 1989): 16–30.

Smith, Frederik N. "Telepathic Diction: Verbal Repetition in *As I Lay Dying*." *Style* 19 (Spring 1985): 66–77.

Tredell, Nicholas, ed. *William Faulkner: The Sound and the Fury and As I Lay Dying*. Columbia Critical Guides. New York: Columbia UP, 1999.

Wadlington, Warwick. *As I Lay Dying: Stories out of Stories*. New York: Twayne, 1992.

Wright, Austin M. *Recalcitrance, Faulkner, and the Professors*. Iowa City: U of Iowa P, 1990.

LIGHT IN AUGUST (1932)

Contemporary Reviews

Adams, J. Donald. "Mr. Faulkner's Astonishing Novel." *New York Times Book Review* October 9, 1932: 6, 24.

Canby, Henry S. "The Grain of Life." *Saturday Review of Literature* October 8, 1932: 153, 156.

Shipman, Evan. *New Republic* 72 (October 26, 1932): 300–01.

Thompson, Alan Reynolds. "The Cult of Cruelty." *Bookman* 74 (January-February 1932): 477–87.

Tyler, Parker. "Book Reviews." *The New Act* 1 (January 1933): 36–39.

Criticism

Benson, Carl. "Thematic Design in *Light in August*." *South Atlantic Quarterly* 53 (October 1954): 540–55.

Berland, Alwyn. Light in August: *A Study in Black and White*. New York: Twayne, 1992.

Bleikasten, André. "*Light in August*: The Closed Society and Its Subjects." In Millgate *New Essays* 81–102.

Collins, R. G. "*Light in August*: Faulkner's Stained Glass Triptych." *Mosaic* 7 (Fall 1973): 97–157.

Cottrell, Beekman W. "Christian Symbols in *Light in August*." *Modern Fiction Studies* 2 (Winter 1956): 207–13.

Godden, Richard. "'Call Me Nigger!': Race and Speech in Faulkner's *Light in August*." *American Studies* 14 (1980): 235–48.

Gold, Joseph. "The Two Worlds of *Light in August*." *Mississippi Quarterly* 16 (Summer 1963): 160–67.

Lind, Ilse Dusoir. "The Calvinistic Burden of *Light in August*." *New England Quarterly* 30 (1957): 307–29.

———. "Apocalyptic Vision as Key to *Light in August*." *Studies in American Fiction* 3 (1975): 133–41.

Millgate, Michael. "'A Novel: Not an Anecdote': Faulkner's *Light in August*." In Millgate *New Essays* 31–53.

———, ed. *New Essays on* Light in August. New York: Cambridge UP, 1987.

Pitavy, François. *Faulkner's* Light in August. Rev. and enlarged ed. Trans. Gillian E. Cook. Bloomington: U of Indiana P, 1973.

———. *William Faulkner's* Light in August: *A Critical Handbook*. New York: Garland, 1982.

Ruppersburg, Hugh M. *Reading Faulkner*: Light in August. Jackson: UP of Mississippi, 1994.

Slabey, Robert M. "Joe Christmas, Faulkner's Marginal Man." *Phylon* 21 (Fall 1960): 266–77.

———. "Myth and Ritual in *Light in August*." *Texas Studies in Literature and Language* 2 (1960): 328–49.

Toomey, David M. "The Human Heart in Conflict: *Light in August*'s Schizophrenic Narrator." *Studies in the Novel* 23 (1991): 452–69.

Torgovnick, Marianna. "Story-telling as Affirmation at the End of *Light in August*." *Closure in the Novel*. Princeton, NJ: Princeton UP, 1981. 157–75.

Tucker, John. "William Faulkner's *Light in August*: Toward a Structuralist Reading." *Modern Language Quarterly* 43 (1982): 138–55.

Tully, Susan Hayes. "Joanna Burden: 'It's the dead folks that do him the damage'." *Mississippi Quarterly* 40 (1987): 355–71.

Urgo, Joseph R. "Menstrual Blood and 'Nigger' Blood: Joe Christmas and the Ideology of Sex and Race." *Mississippi Quarterly* 41 (1988): 391–401.

Watkins, Ralph. "'It was like I was the woman and she was the man': Boundaries, Portals, and Pollution in *Light in August*." *Southern Literary Journal* 26 (1994): 11–24.

Watson, Jay. "Overdoing Masculinity in *Light in August*; or, Joe Christmas and the Gender Guard." *Faulkner Journal* 9 (1993–1994): 149–77.

Welsh, Alexander. "On the Difference Between Prevailing and Enduring." In Millgate *New Essays* 123–47.

Wittenberg, Judith Bryant. "The Women of *Light in August*." In Millgate *New Essays* 103–22.

ABSALOM, ABSALOM! (1936)

Contemporary Reviews

De Voto, Bernard. "Witchcraft in Mississippi." *Saturday Review of Literature* 15 (October 31, 1936): 3–4, 14.

Fadiman, Clifton. "Faulkner, Extra-Special, Double-Distilled." *New Yorker* October 31, 1936: 4-D.

Mann, Dorothy L. "William Faulkner as Self-Conscious Stylist." [Boston] *Evening Transcript* October 31, 1936: 6.

Rahv, Philip. "Faulkner and Destruction." *New Masses* November 24, 1936: 20–21.

Smith, Henry (Nash). "William Faulkner Continues to Depict Decadence of South." [Dallas] *Morning News*, November 29, 1936: II 9.

Criticism

Adamowski, T. H. "Children of the Idea: Heroes and Family Romances in *Absalom, Absalom!*" *Mosaic* 10 (1976): 115–31.

Aswell, Duncan. "The Puzzling Design of *Absalom, Absalom!*" *Kenyon Review* 30 (1968): 67–84.

Bassett, John E. "*Absalom, Absalom!*: The Limits of Narrative Form." *Modern Language Quarterly* 46 (1985): 276–92.

Batty, Nancy E. "The Riddle of *Absalom, Absalom!*: Looking at the Wrong Blackbird." *Mississippi Quarterly* 47 (1994): 461–88.

Behrens, Ralph. "Collapse of Dynasty: The Thematic Center of *Absalom, Absalom!*" *PMLA* 89 (1974): 24–33.

Bloom, Harold, ed. *William Faulkner's* Absalom, Absalom! New York: Chelsea House, 1987.

Boone, Joseph A. "Creation by the Father's Fiat: Paternal Narrative, Sexual Anxiety, and the Deauthorizing Designs of *Absalom, Absalom!*" *Refiguring the Father: New Feminist Readings of Patriarchy*. Ed. Patricia Yaeger and Beth Kowaleski-Wallace. Carbondale: Southern Illinois UP, 1989. 209–37.

Brooks, Peter. "Incredulous Narration: *Absalom, Absalom!*" *Reading for the Plot: Design and Intention in Narrative*. New York: Vintage, 1985. 286–312.

Dalziel, Pamela. "*Absalom, Absalom!*: The Extension of Dialogic Form." *Mississippi Quarterly* 45 (1992): 277–94.

Donaldson, Susan V. "Subverting History: Women, Narrative and Patriarchy in *Absalom, Absalom!*" *Southern Quarterly* 26 (1988): 19–32.

Doody, Terrence. "Shreve McCannon and the Confessions of *Absalom, Absalom!*" *Studies in the Novel* 6 (1974): 454–69.

Egan, Philip J. "Embedded Story Structures in *Absalom, Absalom!*" *American Literature* 55 (1983): 199–214.

Forrer, Richard. "*Absalom, Absalom!*: Story-telling as a Mode of Transcendence." *Southern Literary Journal* 9 (1976): 22–46.

Garfield, Deborah. "To Love as 'Fiery Ancients' Would: Eros, Narrative and Rosa Coldfield in *Absalom, Absalom!*" *Southern Literary Journal* 22 (1989): 61–79.

Godden, Richard. "*Absalom, Absalom!* and Faulkner's Erroneous Dating of the Haitian Revolution." *Mississippi Quarterly* 47 (1994): 489–95.

Goldman, Arnold, ed. *Twentieth Century Interpretations of* Absalom, Absalom! Englewood Cliffs, NJ: Prentice-Hall, 1971.

Hobson, Fred, ed. *William Faulkner's* Absalom, Absalom! New York: Oxford UP, 2003.

Holman, C. Hugh. "*Absalom, Absalom!*: The Historian as Detective." *Sewanee Review* 79 (1971): 542–53.

Jones, Norman W. "Coming Out through History's Hidden Love Letters in *Absalom, Absalom!*" *American Literature* 76.2 (2004): 339–66.

Kauffman, Linda. "Devious Channels of Decorous Ordering: A Lover's Discourse in *Absalom, Absalom!*" *Modern Fiction Studies* 29 (1983): 183–200.

Kinney, Arthur F. *Critical Essays on William Faulkner: The Sutpen Family.* New York: G. K. Hall, 1996.

Krause, David. "Reading Bon's Letter and Faulkner's *Absalom, Absalom!*" *PMLA* 99 (1984), 225–41.

———. "Opening Pandora's Box: Re-Reading Compson's Letter and Faulkner's *Absalom, Absalom!*" *Mississippi Quarterly* 39 (1986): 368–82.

Kuyk, Dirk, Jr. *Sutpen's Design: Interpreting Faulkner's* Absalom, Absalom! Charlottesville: UP of Virginia, 1990.

Levins, Lynn Gartrell. "The Four Narrative Perspectives in *Absalom, Absalom!*" *PMLA* 85 (1970): 35–47.

Liles, Don Merrick. "William Faulkner's *Absalom, Absalom!*: An Exegesis of the Homoerotic Configurations in the Novel." *Journal of Homosexuality* 8 (1983): 99–111.

McGinnis, Adelaide P. "Charles Bon: The New Orleans Myth Made Flesh." In Kinney 221–26.

Miller, J. Hillis. "The Two Relativisms: Point of View and Indeterminacy in the Novel *Absalom, Absalom!*" *Relativism in the Arts.* Ed. Betty Jean Craige. Athens: U of Georgia P, 1983. 148–70.

Montauzon, Christine de. *Faulkner's* Absalom, Absalom! *and Interpretability: The Inexplicable Unseen.* Bern, Switzerland: Peter Lang, 1985.

Muhlenfeld, Elisabeth, ed. *William Faulkner's* Absalom, Absalom!: A Critical Casebook. New York: Garland, 1984.

O'Donnell, Patrick. "Sub Rosa: Voice, Body, and History in *Absalom, Absalom!*" *College Literature* 16 (1989): 28–47.

Parker, Robert Dale. Absalom, Absalom! *The Questioning of Fictions.* Boston: Twayne, 1991.

Schoenberg, Estella. *Old Tales and Talking: Quentin Compson in William Faulkner's Absalom, Absalom! and Related Works.* Jackson: UP of Mississippi, 1977.

Tobin, Patricia. "The Time of Myth and History in *Absalom, Absalom!*" *American Literature* 45 (1973): 252–70.

Torsney, Cheryl B. "The Vampire Motif in *Absalom, Absalom!*" *Southern Review* 20 (1984): 562–69.

Urgo, Joseph R. "*Absalom, Absalom!*: The Movie." *American Literature* 62 (1990): 56–73.

Wagner-Martin, Linda. "Rosa Coldfield as Daughter: Another of Faulkner's Lost Children." In Kinney 227–38.

THE UNVANQUISHED (1938)

Contemporary Reviews

Boyle, Kay. "Tattered Banners." *New Republic* 94 (March 9, 1938): 136–37.

De Voto, Bernard. "Faulkner's South." *Saturday Review of Literature* 17 (February 19, 1938): 5.

Hicks, Granville. "Confederate Heroism." *New Masses* February 22, 1938: 24.

Kazin, Alfred. "In the Shadow of the South's Last Strand." *New York Herald Tribune* February 20, 1938: 5.

Kronenberger, Louis. "Faulkner's Dismal Swamp." *Nation* 146 (February 19, 1938): 212, 214.

Criticism

Akin, Warren, IV. "'Blood and Raising and Background': The Plot of *The Unvanquished.*" *Modern Language Studies* 11 (1980): 3–11.

Beauchamp, Gorman. "*The Unvanquished*: Faulkner's *Oresteia.*" *Mississippi Quarterly* 23 (1970): 273–77.

Donaldson, Susan V. "Dismantling the *Saturday Evening Post* Reader: *The Unvanquished* and Changing 'Horizons of Expectation.'" *Faulkner and Popular Culture: Faulkner and Yoknapatawpha 1988.* Ed. Doreen Fowler and Ann J. Abadie. Jackson: UP of Mississippi, 1990. 179–95.

Dwyer, June. "Feminization, Masculinization, and the Role of the Woman Patriot in *The Unvanquished.*" *The Faulkner Journal* 6 (1991): 55–64.

Frazer, Winifred L. "Faulkner and Womankind—'No Bloody Moon'." *Faulkner and Women: Faulkner and Yoknapatawpha 1985.* Ed. Doreen Fowler and Ann J. Abadie. Jackson: UP of Mississippi, 1986. 162–79.

Gibb, Robert. "Moving Fast Sideways: A Look at Form and Image in *The Unvanquished.*" *Faulkner Journal* 3 (1988): 40–47.

Haynes, Jayne Isbell. "Faulkner's Verbena." *Mississippi Quarterly* 33 (1980): 355–62.

Hinkle, James. "Reading Faulkner's *The Unvanquished.*" *College Literature* 13 (1986): 217–39.

————, and Robert McCoy. *The Unvanquished: Glossary and Commentary.* Jackson: UP of Michigan, 1995.

Knoll, Robert E. "*The Unvanquished* for a Start." *College English* 19 (1958): 338–43.

Lent, John. "Teaching the Cycle of Short Stories." *English Journal* 70 (1981): 55–57.

Lowe, John. "*The Unvanquished:* Faulkner's Nietzschean Skirmish with the Civil War." *Mississippi Quarterly* 46 (1993): 407–36.

Makowsky, Veronica, and Bradley Johnson. "Teaching *The Unvanquished.*" *Teaching Faulkner: Approaches and Methods.* Ed. Stephen Hahn and Robert W. Hamblin. Westport, CT: Greenwood, 2001. 117–23.

Memmott, A. James. "Sartoris Ludens: The Play Element in *The Unvanquished.*" *Mississippi Quarterly* 29 (1976): 375–87.

Roberts, Diane. "A Precarious Pedestal: The Confederate Woman in Faulkner's *The Unvanquished.*" *Journal of American Studies* 26 (1992): 233–46.

Rogers, David. "Shaking Hands: Gestures Toward Race in Faulkner's *The Unvanquished.*" *Mississippi Quarterly* 43 (1990): 335–48.

Tucker, Edward. "Faulkner's Drusilla and Ibsen's Hedda." *Modern Drama* 16 (1973): 157–61.

Yaeger, Patricia. "Faulkner's 'Greek Amphora Priestess': Verbena and Violence in *The Unvanquished.*" *Faulkner and Gender: Faulkner and Yoknapatawpha 1994.* Ed. Donald M. Kartiganer and Ann J. Abadie. Jackson: UP of Mississippi, 1996. 181–96.

SHORT FICTION

Contemporary Reviews

These Thirteen (1931)

Cantwell, Robert. "Faulkner's Thirteen Stories." *New Republic* October 21, 1931: 271.

Hicks, Granville. "Faulkner and the Short Story." *New York Herald Tribune Books* September 27, 1931: 8.

Sherwood, Robert E. "These Thirteen." *Scribner's Magazine* November 1931: 14, 16.

Stallings, Laurence. "Examples of Faulkner's Extraordinary Quality in His Volume of *These Thirteen.*" New York *Sun* September 23, 1931: 29.

Trilling, Lionel. "Mr. Faulkner's World." *Nation* November 4, 1931: 491–92.

Dr. Martino and Other Stories (1934)

Benét, William Rose. "Fourteen Faulkner Stories." *Saturday Review of Literature* 10 (April 21, 1934): 645.

Jack, Peter Monro. "William Faulkner Presents a Mixed Sheaf of Short Stories." New York *Sun* April 16, 1934: 22.

Kronenberger, Louis. "Mr. Faulkner's Short Stories and Other Recent Fiction." *New York Times Book Review* April 22, 1934: 9.

Knight's Gambit (1949)

Chapin, Ruth. "The World of Faulkner." *Christian Science Monitor* December 8, 1949: 20.

Foote, Shelby. "Five Stories, One Novella and Crime Themes Comprise Faulkner's Newest Collection." *Delta Democrat-Times* (Greenville, MS) November 13, 1939: 18.

Olson, Lawrence. "*Knight's Gambit.*" *Furioso* 5 (Winter 1950): 86–88.

Redding, J. Saunders. "*Knight's Gambit* Annoys, Impresses." Providence *Sunday Journal* November 13, 1949: VI, 8.

Three Famous Short Novels (1958)

Coleman, Philip Y. "Debt Repaid to Faulkner." *Daily Illini* (Champaign, IL) May 13, 1958: n.p.

Criticism

"A Rose for Emily" (1930)

Allen, Dennis W. "Horror and Perverse Delight: Faulkner's 'A Rose for Emily'." *Modern Fiction Studies* 30 (1984): 685–96.

Curry, Renee R. "Gender and Authorial Limitation in Faulkner's 'A Rose for Emily'." *Mississippi Quarterly* 47 (1994): 391–402.

Holland, Norman N. "Fantasy and Defense in Faulkner's 'A Rose for Emily'." *Hartford Studies in Literature* 4 (1972): 1–35.

Inge, M. Thomas, ed. *William Faulkner: A Rose for Emily.* The Merrill Literary Casebook Series. Columbus, OH: Charles E. Merrill, 1970.

Menakhem, Perry. "Literary Dynamics: How the Order of a Text Creates Its Meaning." *Poetics Today* 1 (1979): 35–64, 311–61.

Scherting, Jack. "Emily Grierson's Oedipus Complex: Motif, Motive, and Meaning in Faulkner's 'A Rose for Emily'." *Studies in Short Fiction* 17 (1980): 397–405.

Skinner, John L. "'A Rose for Emily': Against Interpretation." *Journal of Narrative Technique* 15 (1985): 42–51.

Sullivan, Ruth. "The Narrator in 'A Rose for Emily'." *Journal of Narrative Technique* 1 (1971): 159–78.

"That Evening Sun" (1931)

Bennett, Ken. "The Language of the Blues in Faulkner's 'That Evening Sun'." *Mississippi Quarterly* 38 (1985): 339–42.

Brown, May Cameron. "Voice in 'That Evening Sun': A Study of Quentin Compson." *Mississippi Quarterly* 29 (1976): 347–60.

Garrison, Joseph M., Jr. "The Past and the Present in 'That Evening Sun'." *Studies in Short Fiction* 13 (1976): 371–73.

Gartner, Carol B. "Faulkner in Context: Seeing 'That Evening Sun' through the Blues." *Southern Quarterly* 34 (1996): 50–58.

Hamblin, Robert W. "Before the Fall: The Theme of Innocence in Faulkner's 'That Evening Sun'." *Notes on Mississippi Writers* 11 (1979): 86–94.

Johnston, Kenneth G. "The Year of Jubilee: Faulkner's 'That Evening Sun'." *American Literature* 46 (1974): 93–100.

Kuyk, Dirk, Jr., Betty M. Kuyk, and James A. Miller. "Black Culture in William Faulkner's 'That Evening Sun'." *Journal of American Studies* 20 (1986): 33–50.

Momberger, Philip. "Faulkner's 'The Village' and 'That Evening Sun': The Tale in Context." *Southern Literary Journal* 11 (1978): 20–31.

Peek, Charles A. "'Handy' Ways to Teach 'That Evening Sun'." *Teaching Faulkner: Approaches and Methods*. Ed. Stephen Hahn and Robert W. Hamblin. Westport, CT: Greenwood, 2001. 53–58.

Perrine, Laurence. "'That Evening Sun': A Skein of Uncertainties." *Studies in Short Fiction* 22 (1985): 295–307.

Pitcher, E. W. "Motive and Metaphor in Faulkner's 'That Evening Sun'." *Studies in Short Fiction* 18 (1981): 131–35.

Slabey, Robert M. "Faulkner's Nancy as 'Tragic Mulatto'." *Studies in Short Fiction* 27 (1990): 409–13.

Sunderman, Paula. "Speech Act Theory and Faulkner's 'That Evening Sun'." *Language and Style: An International Journal* 14 (1981): 304–14.

"Turnabout" (1932)

Bradford, M. E. "The Anomaly of Faulkner's World War I Stories." *Mississippi Quarterly* 36 (Summer 1983): 243–61.

Hulsey, Dallas. "'I don't seem to remember a girl in the story': Hollywood's Disruption of Faulkner's All-Male Narrative in *Today We Live*." *Faulkner Journal* 16 (2000–2001): 65–77.

Ramsay, D. Matthew. "'Turnabout' is Fair(y) Play: Faulkner's Queer War Story." *Faulkner Journal* 15 (1999–2000): 61–82.

"Barn Burning" (1939)

Billinglea, Oliver. "Fathers and Sons: The Spiritual Quest in Faulkner's 'Barn Burning.'" *Mississippi Quarterly* 44 (1991): 287–308.

Bradford, M. E. "Family and Community in Faulkner's 'Barn Burning'." *The Southern Review* 17 (1981): 332–39.

Cackett, Kathy. "'Barn Burning': Debating the American Adam." *Notes on Mississippi Writers* 21 (1989): 1–17.

Fabijancic, Tony. "Reification, Dereification, Subjectivity: Towards a Marxist Reading of William Faulkner's Poor-White Topography." *Faulkner Journal* 10 (1994): 75–94.

Fowler, Virginia C. "Faulkner's 'Barn Burning': Sarty's Conflict Reconsidered." *College Language Association Journal* 24 (1981): 513–22.

Franklin, Phyllis. "Sarty Snopes and 'Barn Burning'." *Mississippi Quarterly* 21 (1968): 189–93.

Hiles, Jane. "Kinship and Heredity in Faulkner's 'Barn Burning'." *Mississippi Quarterly* 38 (1985): 329–37.

Rio-Jelliffe, R. "The Language of Time in Fiction: A Model in Faulkner's 'Barn Burning'." *Journal of Narrative Technique* 24 (1994): 98–113.

Skaggs, Merrill Maguire. "Story and Film in 'Barn Burning': The Difference a Camera Makes." *Southern Quarterly* 21 (1983): 5–15.

Yunis, Susan S. "The Narrator of Faulkner's 'Barn Burning'." *Faulkner Journal* 6 (1991): 23–31.

Zender, Karl F. "Character and Symbol in 'Barn Burning'." *College Literature* 16 (1989): 48–59.

"Tomorrow" (1940)

Lahey, Michael E. "Trying Emotions: Unpredictable Justice in Faulkner's 'Smoke' and 'Tomorrow'." *Mississippi Quarterly* 46 (1993): 447–62.

Yellin, David G., and Marie Connors, eds. *Tomorrow and Tomorrow and Tomorrow*. Jackson: UP of Mississippi, 1985.

Three Famous Short Novels (1958)

Spotted Horses

Eddins, Dwight. "Metahumor in 'Spotted Horses'." *Ariel* 13 (1982): 23–31.

Heck, Francis. "Faulkner's 'Spotted Horses': A Variation of a Rabelaisian Theme." *Arizona Quarterly* 37 (1981): 166–72.

Houghton, Donald E. "Whores and Horses in Faulkner's 'Spotted Horses'." *Midwest Quarterly* 11 (1970): 361–69.

Ramsay, Allen. "'Spotted Horses' and Spotted Pups." *Faulkner Journal* 2 (1990): 35–38.

Rankin, Elizabeth D. "Chasing Spotted Horses: The Quest for Human Dignity in Faulkner's Snopes Trilogy." *Faulkner: The Unappeased Imagination: A Collection of Critical Essays*. Ed. Glenn O. Carey. Troy, NY: Whitston, 1980.

Old Man

Cumpiano, Marion W. "The Motif of Return: Currents and Counter Currents in 'Old Man' by William Faulkner." *Southern Humanities Review* 12 (1978): 185–93.

Feaster, John. "Faulkner's *Old Man*: A Psychoanalytic Approach." *Modern Fiction Studies* 13 (1967): 89–94.

Fowler, Doreen A. "Measuring Faulkner's Tall Convict." *Studies in the Novel* 14 (1982): 280–84.

McHaney, Thomas L. *William Faulkner's The Wild Palms: A Study*. Southern Literature Series. Jackson: UP of Mississippi, 1975.

Samway, Patrick, S. J. "A Revisionist's Approach to Faulkner's 'Old Man'." *Les Cahiers de la Nouvelle* 1 (1983): 113–26.

Taylor, Nancy Dew. "The River of Faulkner and Twain." *Mississippi Quarterly* 16 (1963): 191–99.

Turner, W. Craig. "Faulkner's 'Old Man' and the American Humor Tradition." *University of Mississippi Studies in English* 5 (1984–1987): 149–57.

The Bear

Beauchamp, Gorman. "The Rite of Initiation in Faulkner's 'The Bear'." *Arizona Quarterly* 28 (1972): 319–25.

Claridge, Laura P. "Isaac McCaslin's Failed Bid for Adulthood." *American Literature* 55 (1983): 241–51.

Godden, Richard, and Noel Polk. "Reading the Ledgers." *Mississippi Quarterly* 55 (2002): 301–59.

Harrison, Robert. "Faulkner's 'The Bear': Some Notes on Form." *Georgia Review* 20 (Fall 1966), 318–27.

Howell, Elmo. "Faulkner's Elegy: An Approach to 'The Bear'." *Arlington Quarterly* 2 (1969–70): 122–32.

Jensen, Eric G., Jr. "The Play Element in Faulkner's 'The Bear'." *Texas Studies in Literature and Language* 5 (1964): 170–87.

Kinney, Arthur F. *"Go Down, Moses": The Miscegenation of Time*. New York: Twayne, 1996.

Lewis, R.W.B. "The Hero in the New World: William Faulkner's 'The Bear.'" *Kenyon Review* 13 (1951): 641–60.

McGee, Patrick. "Gender and Generation in Faulkner's 'The Bear.'" *Faulkner Journal* 1 (1985): 46–54.

Nestrick, William V. "The Function of Form in 'The Bear,' Section IV." *Twentieth Century Literature* 12 (1966): 131–37.

Rudich, Norman. "Faulkner and the Sin of Private Property." *Minnesota Review* 17 (1981), 55–57.

Utley, Francis Lee, Lynn Z. Bloom, and Arthur F. Kinney, eds. *Bear, Man, and God : Seven Approaches to William Faulkner's 'The Bear.'* New York: Random House, 1964.

Warren, Joyce W. "The Role of Lion in Faulkner's 'The Bear': Key to a Better Understanding." *Arizona Quarterly* 24 (1968): 252–60.

RELATED SECONDARY SOURCES

Althusser, Louis. "Ideology and Ideological State Apparatuses." *Literary Theory: An Anthology.* Ed. Julie Rivkin and Michael Ryan. Malden, MA: Blackwell, 1998. 295–304.

Booth, Wayne. *The Rhetoric of Fiction.* 2nd ed. Chicago: U of Chicago P, 1983.

Carlson, Marvin. *Performance: A Critical Introduction.* 2nd ed. New York: Routledge, 2004.

Fiedler, Leslie A. *Love and Death in the American Novel.* New rev. ed. New York: Laurel, 1969.

Gramsci, Antonio. "Hegemony." *Literary Theory: An Anthology.* Ed. Julie Rivkin and Michael Ryan. Malden, MA: Blackwell, 1998. 277.

Humphrey, Robert. *Stream of Consciousness in the Modern Novel.* Berkeley: U of California P, 1954.

Long, Beverly Whitaker, and Mary Frances HopKins. *Performing Literature: An Introduction.* Dubuque, IA: Kendall/Hunt, 1997.

Madison, D. Soyini, and Judith Hamera, eds. *The SAGE Handbook of Performance Studies.* Thousand Oaks, CA: Sage, 2006.

Malpas, Simon. "Historicism." *The Routledge Companion to Critical Theory.* Ed. Simon Malpas and Paul Wake. New York: Routledge, 2006. 55–65.

Martin, Wallace. *Some Recent Theories of Narrative.* Ithaca, NY: Cornell UP, 1986.

Radway, Janice. *Reading the Romance: Women, Patriarchy, and Popular Literature.* Chapel Hill: U of North Carolina P, 1984.

Rivkin, Julie, and Michael Ryan. "Starting with Zero: Basic Marxism." *Literary Theory: An Anthology.* Ed. Julie Rivkin and Michael Ryan. Malden, MA: Blackwell, 1998. 231–242.

Schechner, Richard. *Performance Studies: An Introduction.* 2nd ed. New York: Routledge, 2006.

Index

About the Author

JOHN DENNIS ANDERSON is associate professor of organizational and political communication and former Honors Program director at Emerson College. A performance studies scholar and past chair of the Performance Studies Division of the National Communication Association, he presents Chautauqua performances throughout the country as Henry James, William Faulkner, and Washington Irving. His performance as the Native American playwright Lynn Riggs was part of the Oklahoma Centennial Chautauqua in 2007.